AF538292

DANIEL:

THE VISION OF THE END

Revised Edition

"Prophecy is a moment of unshrouding, an opening of the eyes, a lifting of the curtain."

Abraham Heschel, *The Prophets*, pp. 193-194

DANIEL: THE VISION OF THE END

JACQUES B. DOUKHAN

Andrews University Press  Berrien Springs, Mi

Andrews University Press
Sutherland House
Berrien Springs, MI 49104-1700
Telephone: 269-471-6134
FAX: 269-471-6224
Email: aupo@andrews.edu
Website: http://www.universitypress.andrews.edu

Copyright © 1987 by Jacques B. Doukhan

All rights reserved. No part of this book may be used or reproduced in any manner or translated into other languages without written permission except in the case of brief quotations embodied in critical articles and reviews.

Printed in the United States of America

12 11 10 09 08 10 9 8 7 6

ISBN: 978-0-943872-41-4

Library of Congress Catalog Card Number: 87-82339

CONTENTS

CHAPTER TWO

CHAPTER THREE

CHAPTER FOUR

PREFACE

The end has given birth to this book.

A personal and dramatic experience with death, combined with the end of a period in my life, has marked the conception of this work. On the other hand, beyond the personal experience, symptoms of crisis and of decomposition in the world are offered everywhere to the lucid observer. The end is no more a strange concept or a mere doctrine brandished by some obscure sect; today men of all sides shout and warn, and begin to tremble for their city.[1]

Alongside this existential reference, and *not because of* it, the Bible also happens to point to the end. This is the conclusion I have come to after several years of wrestling with the prophetic word.[2]

Now, besides the consciousness this first lesson may teach, it also conveys a subsequent requirement for the reader of the Bible; if indeed the Bible points to the end, it invites then to a special place in the book which, more than any other in the Bible, focuses on the end, namely, the book of Daniel. The study of this particular book would not be dictated then by a doctrinal statement, a scholarly task, or some personal predilection for the apocalyptic universe. Instead, it is motivated by the whole word of the Bible. Rather than being just a peculiar and isolated book within biblical literature, the book of Daniel would then constitute the ultimate step to which the Bible leads.

Furthermore, besides being the most eschatological book in comparison to others in the Bible, the book of Daniel is in itself essentially concerned with the time of the end. As we shall demonstrate, the written space which is devoted to the end, the key words, the structure of the book indicate this emphasis. In this sense, one may say that the book of Daniel is, so to speak, the Bible in a microcosm. One should have expected it to be so, not only because, like the whole Bible, it points to the end, but also because it *is* the book of the end. This is the awareness which strikes anyone when reaching the end: as in a flash every force, every pulsation, every event is collected to bring out the ultimate vision. Thus, the end is "seen." The prophet describes it as a Vision of Judgment, a Vision of Waiting, a Vision of War. Successively each aspect of this Vision will be explored throughout the book of Daniel, thus obliging us to enter it from three different perspectives. The whole picture which reaches us over the centuries is both strange and familiar: an apocalyptic and fantastic picture arises, and finally turns our nightmare into an unexpected vision of hope--the Vision of Michael. At that stage we shall pause and reflect on this unbelievable event which closes the human adventure. The specific nature of the content has thus somewhat affected the tone of the last section. After struggling with the biblical text and sometimes demanding close attention, the study will slow down into a rather spiritual meditation, in the wake of Daniel's lessons. Moreover, in order not to disrupt the logic of the demonstration or flow of the discourse, I have chosen as far as possible to present the significant scholarly discussion in the footnotes.

I have proceeded under the pressure of two conjoint realities. On one hand sticking to the book of the prophet, I was led to center my investigations on the vision of the end; the biblical text implies the necessity of this attention. I have thus followed the movement of the text rather than treat specific problems separately and systematically. Consequently the material was progressively unfolded and, part by part, in the manner of a puzzle, the whole picture came out. This justifies an important warning here: only at the end of the process will the reader fully understand, and sometimes along the way, he may feel frustrated--but this very procedure is dictated by the method of the prophet Daniel himself, this being his pedagogy. On the other hand, both existential experience and history have come from outside to meet this biblical concern of the end urging a *committed* study of the prophetic word. It is therefore not only as a biblical interpreter, but also as a man in the flesh that I have conducted this work after a method I shall define in due course. Facing the end, the scholar and the man cannot be dissociated. Personal reflections, then, will be intertwined with this exegetical study insofar as the book of Daniel has something relevant to say about human destiny.

INTRODUCTION

"Understand son of man that the vision refers to the time of the end."

Daniel 8:17

Before venturing into the book, it is our duty to determine the nature of the path which will lead us to its understanding. In a first step we shall draw the theological emphasis and perspective of the book, in order to be ready for the second step, to delineate our methodology accordingly. Thus, our methodology and interpretation, instead of coming from outside with philosophical presuppositions, will endeavor to move from within the clues provided by the book itself.

The Eschatological Perspective of the Book of Daniel

The book of Daniel is the biblical book which, more than any other, refers to the end, and is consequently the most eschatological book of the Old Testament. The statistics, the way the book begins and ends, and its literary structure eloquently testify to the eschatological emphasis of the book of Daniel.

Statistics

The statistics are particularly telling on this point. Out of the thirty-two biblical occurences of the Hebrew word *qēṣ* (end), fourteen come from the book of Daniel, nine from Ezekiel and Jeremiah, five from Genesis, four from Isaiah. Also, out of the eight occurences of the Aramaic word *sôp̱* (end), five come from the book of Daniel, two from Ecclesiastes, and one from 2 Chronicles. While this strong reference to the end pervading the whole book testifies to its unity, it also indicates how intensely concerned this book is, more than any other in the Bible,[3] with "the time of the end" (Daniel 12:4, 9).

Literary Frame

Furthermore, besides just being the most eschatological book in comparison to others in the Bible, Daniel is also in itself, whether it deals with actual history or with prophecy, essentially concerned with the end. It is significant that the book of Daniel is literally framed with references to the end. The book opens with a catastrophe, the exile of Israel, the end of a nation (Daniel 1:1); it closes with the personal end of Daniel himself in relation to the absolute end of the world (Daniel 12:13). One enters and leaves the book with the same taste of death and of tragic end. The device is pedagogical. It tells us that the end of universal history and the end of this particular history are connected, thereby suggesting that they belong to the same line; both are of the same "historico-eschatological" vein.

Literary Structure

This "historico-eschatological" character is strongly suggested in *the literary structure* of the book of Daniel. Recent studies on this subject have pointed out the existence of a so-called "concentric parallelism" tying the aramaic chapters: 2 and 7; 3 and 6; 4 and 5.[4] I propose to go further and be attentive to the same phenomenon in the rest of the book, namely 7 and 12; 8 and 11; 9 and 10.[5] Indeed these chapters offer the same picture of "concentric parallelism" just as in the first half of the book. The connection between the respective chapters is not only made of specific features which characterize them apart from other chapters but also pertains to the whole chapters themselves, on the structural level.

Chapter 7 is related to chapter 12 on the motif of the Judgment and the Parousia; these are the only passages where the evocation of Judgment and the books of the saved are associated with the coming of a specific Individual called "the Son of Man" in Dan. 7 or Michael in Dan. 12. Remarkable also is the fact that the first prophetic period mentioned in chapter 12 is precisely the one which is pointed out in chapter 7, namely "a time, times, and half a time" (12:7; cf. 7:25). Moreover, chapter 7 and chapter 12 are connected along a chiastic pattern ($ABC//C_1B_1A_1$):

	Ch 7:		Ch 12:
A	little horn and "a time, times, and half a time" (7:24-25)	C_1	Michael (12:1a)
B	Judgment (7:9-12; cf. 26)	B_1	Judgment (12:1b-3)
C	Son of Man (7:13-14)	A_1	little horn (7:13-14) and "a time, times, and half a time (12:4-13)

Chapter 8 is related to chapter 11 on the specific motif of a conflict; these are the only passages where history is described in terms of a fight: chapter 8 tells us about the fight of a ram and a goat, and chapter 11 tells us about the fight of the North and the South. Both chapters tell us about a two-level conflict: on one level opposing pagan powers (8:1-9, 20-21; cf. 11:1-14) and on the other level opposing the power of usurpation to the saints and the holy mountain (8:10-14, 23-26; cf. 11:22, 30-35, 45). Moreover chapter 8 and 11 are written in parallelism and progress in four steps along the same movement ABCD // $A_1B_1C_1D_1$:

	Ch. 8		Ch. 11
A	fight between Persia and Greece (vv. 1-8)	A_1	fight between Persia and Greece (vv. 1-4a)
B	Rome is implied* (v. 9)	B_1	Rome is implied* (v. 4b)
C	struggles of the power of usurpation (vv. 10-13, 23-25)	C_1	struggles of the power of usurpation (vv. 5-39)
D	the time of the end (vv. 14, 26)	D_1	the time of the end (vv. 40-45a)
E	the Advent: "he shall be broken without human hand" (v. 25b)	E_1	the Advent: "he shall come to his end and no one will help him" (v. 45b)

Chapter 9 is related to chapter 10 especially on the specific motif of "weeks," (9:24-27; cf. 10:2, 3)[6] but essentially on the deeper

---

*For the implied presence of Rome see the treatment of the respective passages in the interpretation of ch. 8 and 11.

level of the structure; both progress in parallel following the same three steps, ABC // $A_1B_1C_1$:

	Ch. 9		Ch. 10
A	Daniel "understands" a revealed message (v. 1)	A_1	Daniel "understands" a revealed message (v. 1)
B	prayer of repentance and fasting (vv. 2-17)	B_1	prayer of repentance and fasting (vv. 2-3)
C	vision given as a response to "the prayer which was heard from the beginning" (vv. 20-27, esp. v. 22)	C_1	vision given as a response to "the prayer which was heard from the beginning" (vv. 4-21, esp. v. 12)

Thus, the whole book of Daniel follows a pattern. This observation not only testifies on behalf of its organic unity, but also indicates that the historical and the prophetic are deeply connected. In fact, the connection between the historical section (ch. 2-6) and the prophetic section (ch. 7-12) is not only observed through the literary device of parallelisms, but works also on the level of their respective content. The historical chapters are also eschatologically oriented just as the prophetic chapters are also historically oriented. In the historical section every chapter attests a future orientation beyond the actual history, a waiting for hope, a hint to the end (ch. 2:44-45; 3:17-18; 4:34-37; 5:23-28; 6:26). In the prophetic section every chapter is enrooted in history (7:1; 8:1; 9:1; 10:1; 11:1) and the prophecy which is supposed to bring the hope of the end is systematically situated by reference to history (7:17-18; 8:20-26; 3:2, 24-27; 10:13-14; 11:2-4, 45; 12:13).

As for chapter 1, it plays the function of the general introduction to the whole book. It contains not only all the theological concepts of the book but it contains, and thereby announces, the general motif of the book. Here also the historical and the prophetic are intertwined. The concern of the end[7] pervades the chapter and beyond the historical event, it indicates the three theological motifs of judgment, waiting and war, which characterize the whole book of Daniel. Moreover, the way this chapter begins and ends is significant of the intention of its author; it opens with reference to the tragedy of exile, and closes with reference to Cyrus, who puts an end to the exile (2 Ch. 36:22, 25). In other words, chapter 1 indicates, on the threshold of the book, that prophecy is not just a game of the mind, a mere piece of poetry; it has to do with concrete history. Chapter 1 tells us that from history's point of view—Daniel is in the time of Cyrus when he writes chapter 1 (v. 21)—prophecy is to be fulfilled. Prophecy points to an historical event. This is the message of chapter 1. This is also the very message which is conveyed through the literary structure of the whole book as it discloses the deep connections tying the two sections together.

The picture of the structure may be represented in two ways:

1. Concentric Parallels

ch. 1 2 3 4 5 6 7 8 9 10 11 12

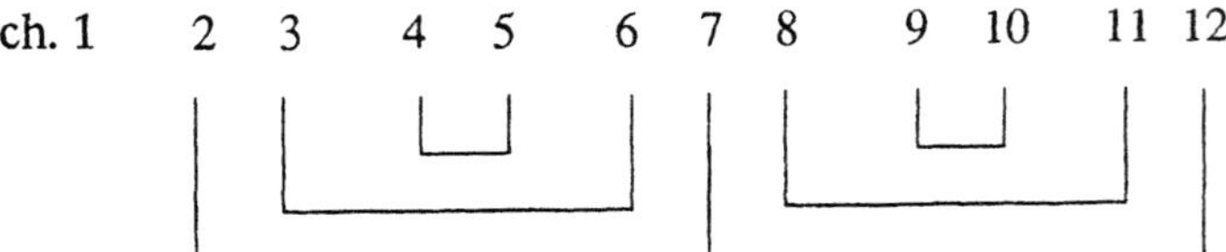

2. Chiastic Structure

ch. 1

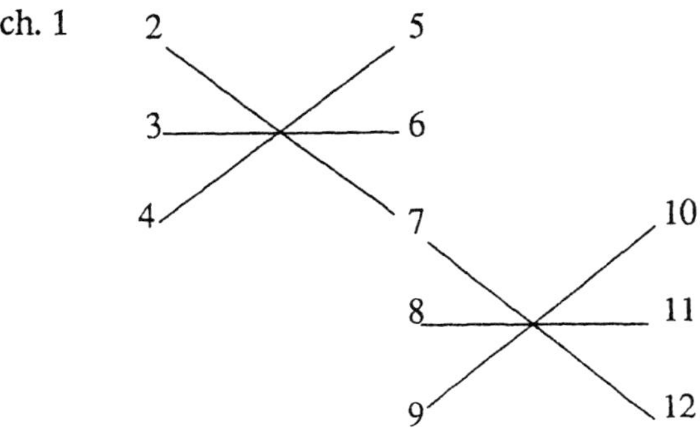

Another indication of this particular emphasis is the fact that in the chapters dealing with the whole course of human history, an important proportion of verses are concerned with the end.

In chapter 2, five verses (41-45) out of the nine (37-45) deal with the end; in chapter 7, five verses (24-28) out of the eight (17, 18, 23-28); in chapter 8, four verses (23-26) out of the seven (20-26); in chapter 11, forty verses (5-45) out of the forty-five;[8] and in chapter 12, thirteen verses (1-13) out of the thirteen. This movement is significant. On one hand the emphasis on history parallels a particular focus on the end. On the other hand the emphasis on the end goes along with the focus on human history.

Therefore, the "eschatological" emphasis is not only designed to make one aware of the importance of the end, but also to underline its historical reality. The time of the end is not a vague theological concept, or, as some claim,[9] a comforting thought invented by a suffering people. The time of the end is set up by Daniel in the reality of human history. Indeed, propelled by his vision beyond the centuries, the prophet dares to situate the time of the end with regard to the whole universal history, and goes so far as to date the last step.

Methodology

This double-featured character of Daniel's prophecies, namely their profound incarnation in history and their strong orientation toward the end, invites a specific method of interpretation which we shall now define and situate with regard to other approaches.

Various Approaches

Three main systems have marked the history of interpretation of these prophecies.

1. The "preterist" approach interprets prophecy by reference to past events. It claims that the book of Daniel was written against the background of contemporary events, in this instance the oppression of Antiochus Epiphanes (175-164 B.C.). According to these interpreters, the book of Daniel is a work of fiction

written during the Maccabean period to encourage resistance against tyranny. This position is held by the vast majority of modern commentators and critical scholars who repudiate the "miracle" of the prediction and prefer the more reasonable and elegant *vaticinium ex eventu.*[10]

2. The "futurist" approach is practically the reverse of the former and projects all prophecies into the future, hence beyond our control. A classical example of these interpretations can be found in the so-called "dispensationalist" system,[11] especially as it deals with the 70 weeks of Daniel 9:24-27. It is taught, for example, that a gap of about 20 centuries intervenes between the end of the 69th week at Christ's death and the 70th week at the time of the end. It is also noteworthy that some Christian theologians may be futurists and emphasize the eschatological fulfillment of the prophecy without, however, accepting the whole dispensationalist view.[12]

3. The "historicist" approach interprets prophecy with regard to historical events from the time the prophecy was uttered down to the end of time. This is likely to be the most ancient system of interpretation (in both Jewish and Christian traditions).[13] This latter method is so far the only one which respects the historical intention of the biblical author as such. The "preterist" approach makes the Bible lie, the "futurist" approach makes the Bible a work of science fiction; neither one seriously takes the historical data into account. An unfortunate tendency is to be noted, however, among those who hold the "historicist" approach. Out of the concern to relate the prophecy to the event, they have often overlooked the reality of the biblical text. Instead of starting from the text, they have come to the text out of the historical or political event. Thus, the language of the prophet, his world of thought, his literary and historical settings have been ignored in most cases. Some have gone so far as to substitute themselves for the prophet and even guess the event to come—hence the numerous discrepancies and the strange applications which have discredited this approach.[14] Besides, this approach has often failed to notice the eschatological orientation of the prophecies.

Our Method

Our method proceeds with elements of truth found in each of the three methods. With the "historicists" we will search the fulfillment of prophecy on the level of history. With the "preterists" we will share the concern to meet the prophet where he is, in his language and in his world. With the "futurists" we will not ignore the eschatological accent of the prophecy. This does not mean, however, that we hold the three systems as entirely valuable. Actually the three systems cannot be used together. A single prophecy does not have several applications, as has been asserted in the so-called "apotelesmatic" approach.[15] If one prophecy happens to point to different historical times, it is simply because the events are "seen" in the same perspective—following the linear Hebrew conception of time.[16] This is, for example, the case of Matthew 24, which obviously sets the end of Jerusalem and the end of the world in the same perspective. But here also the exegesis must work under the control of the text to make sure that this multifold application is indeed intended by the biblical author. In fact, this type of prophecy could hardly be found in the book of Daniel for the simple reason that the predicted events are there carefully located in time. Both the sequence within the flow of history and the numbers which date the predicted events provide enough security to ensure a clear-cut distinction between them, even though the author may relate them by putting them in the same perspective (see our treatment of Daniel 8 and 9).

Our approach is thus essentially "exegetical;" we start from within the text with all the risk this task implies—*with faith*. The latter remark indicates another element of our approach. We want to take the prophetic text at its word, in its explicit lesson as well as in its implicit, yet intended, allusions and associations. We want not only to be attentive to its linguistic, literary and historical data,[17] but also to its setting within the wider framework of the "inspired" book.[18]

Finally, since prophecy and history are essentially related in the book of Daniel, it appeals for a specific hermeneutic. We want to take the prophetic text at its word while looking through history in order to check whether, indeed, the prophet "has seen well" (Jer. 1:12). Thus our methodology follows the very lines indicated by the text itself. Besides, this information is precious, for not only will it enable us to situate our "history" in history, but also by the same token to situate our time and ourselves in regard to the time of the end. It is a "symptomatic" time which has been described by the prophet Daniel as a time of preparation for the coming of Michael. The vision of the end is therefore a Vision of Judgment, a Vision of Waiting, and a Vision of War. It is a Judgment, because on God's level it is the preparation for the heavenly Kingdom, a Waiting because on the human level it is the preparation for the heavenly Kingdom, and a War because on a cosmic level–involving God and the nations–it is the preparation for the heavenly Kingdom.

CHAPTER ONE

A VISION OF JUDGMENT

"And a judgment was made in favor of the saints."

Daniel 7:22

The name Daniel hints at the profound vocation of his book. Daniel means literally "*my judge* (is) God," with an emphasis on judge.[19] Indeed, the event of the judgment lies at the heart of his interest,[20] and it is not a coincidence that chapter 7, "the core of the book,"[21] is mainly concerned with the judgment.

Not only the middle of the book but also its two extremities point to judgment. In the beginning, judgment is suggested when the hand of God is profiled behind the exile, which tragically brings the end of Israel. "The Lord gave Jehoiakim King of Judah into his hands . . ." (Daniel 1:2). Also at the end of the book the idea of judgment is pointed out by reference to the *goral,*[22] the eschatological retribution awaiting Daniel (Daniel 12:13). The motif of judgment can be traced everywhere throughout the book of Daniel.

Judgment is in chapter 1 when "at the end of the days" (1:18) a test resulted in the superiority of the Hebrews over all the magicians and astrologers (1:15, 19-20). In a similar way chapters 3 and 6 tell us about the testing experience from which the three Hebrews (ch. 3) and Daniel (ch. 6) are rescued. The result is always the same, bearing a double effect: death for the pagans and salvation and promotion for Daniel and his camp, showing that God is the judge of both.

Judgment is also a part of the texture of chapter 2 which conveys the idea of a "God of heaven" who is in control (2:29-30, 37), who "removes kings and raises up kings" (2:21), who possesses every wisdom (2:20), and knows every secret (2:18, 19, 22, 27, 29, 47, etc.). All these key notions are generally associated in order to convey the idea of a God above who watches over the earth in the perspective of judgment. Being the "God of Heaven" God is also the Judge; and this association of thoughts prepares one for the heavenly judgment scene (ch. 7).

Chapter 4 also shows a God who watches from above (4:13), a God who "rules the Kingdom of men" (4:17) and controls history. This is the lesson of the tree which is chopped down and cut off by a decree of God (4:17). This is also the lesson which is contained in Nebuchadnezzar's dramatic experience. As the king was walking about the royal palace of Babylon, praising himself and his own works, suddenly a voice sounded from heaven and the king became like an animal (4:33). "At the end of the time" (v. 34) when Nebuchadnezzar repents, he finally understands that "God does according to His will in the army of heaven" (4:35). Similarly chapter 5 tells us about a pagan king[23] who is surprised in the course of his sin. The judgment motif is particularly embedded in chapter 5. The hand which suddenly appears to Belshazzar, who is praising the gods of metal, reminds him that he has not glorified the "God who holds your breath in his hand and owns all your ways" (5:23). Furthermore, the writing hand on the wall conveys in itself a reference to judgment; the latter event is usually associated with the act of writing (7:10; 12:1). The judgment implies the "written" record of men's actions in the book. For Belshazzar the fact that the hand is writing means his judgment.[24] Now, the words of the inscription are themselves loaded with judgment. "*Menē, menē, tekēl, ûparsîn*" (v. 25). "Your kingdom has been numbered" (v. 26). "You have been weighed and found wanting" (v. 27). "Your kingdom has been divided and given to . . ." (v. 28). Indeed, all these motifs belong to the language of judgment.[25] Moreover, the fact that the inscription is expressed in the rhythm of four words, although there are only three different words (one is repeated), conveys the specific intention of reminding this king that his kingdom has been numbered and that the end has come.[26] The words spoke not only through their meaning but also through the rhythm of the phrase. The latter lesson will be repeated over and over again in the more universal vision of the four earthly kingdoms (cf. especially ch. 2 and 7).

In chapters 7 and 8, as we shall see, the eschatological event of the judgment is brought to the forefront of the visions. In chapter 7 it is the heavenly scene of the Day of Judgment; in chapter 8 it is the heavenly scene of the Day of Atonement.

Both chapters 9 and 10 tell us about Daniel's experience of judgment in terms of fasting, repentance and prayer. On the horizon stands the figure of a heavenly High Priest (10:5), and the whole section culminates with an explicit reference to the judgment. The book is open (12:1).

The perspective of judgment is indeed at the heart of the book, but it is also in the heart of men—Daniel, his companions, and the kings who are the heroes of these accounts. This does not mean that the judgment functions as a mere existential experience. Rather the various personal experiences of men convey a specific lesson. Great historical events, as well as our tiny existences, are *examined* and will one day have to stand before the judgment. Actually, these two notions are essentially connected. The times are numbered and therefore the Day of Judgment has been precisely located in history and marked in time. It falls within the sequence of the universal kingdoms, represented in chapter 2 by a statue and in chapters 7 and 8 by beasts. It falls, too, within the lines of a prophetic calendar set up on the basis of chronological information provided by chapter 9.

The Statue of Destiny (Daniel 2)

No wonder the Babylonian king dreams of a statue. His world is crowded with them. The astrologers of those times were fond of representing the cosmos and universal history through a statue of a man.[27]

If Nebuchadnezzar erects a statue of himself in his country (ch. 3), it is because he wants to impose upon the minds of his people the idea of his own power over destiny and history. But, the statue of a man that Nebuchadnezzar is dreaming of does not seem to fit the idea he entertains of his own history and destiny. He is greatly disturbed "as if he already had some inkling of its portentous importance."[28] He therefore dares not assume it but seems to flee from the dream by forgetting it.[29]

> I have dreamed a dream; and my spirit is troubled on knowing the dream (v. 3).

Four Kingdoms

To his amazement, the statue is composed of several materials which decrease in value as he looks from the head to the feet. Those materials are not only used to suggest decadence (from gold to clay), they also have a function of representation. Each material is designed to convey a specific characteristic of the kingdom it stands for. This principle is explicit with regard to the iron, for example, "and the fourth kingdom shall be as strong as iron, inasmuch as iron breaks in pieces" (2:40).

Indeed, Nebuchadnezzar has good reason to worry. History will not stop at Babylon. After Babylon (605-539 B.C.), the head of gold (v. 37), comes Medo-Persia (539-331 B.C.), the chest and arms of silver (v. 37a; cf. 5:26-28). Then comes Greece (331-146 B.C.), the belly and thighs of bronze (v. 39b; cf. 8:21) and then Rome (146 B.C.-476 A.D.), the legs of iron (v. 40).[30]

A Fifth Kingdom

Finally the vision reaches its ultimate step, which demands the greatest attention from the prophet (more than half of the text is devoted to it), the feet partly of iron and partly of clay. This curious motif receives three different meanings in the prophecy.

First, the association of iron and clay is interpreted on the level of general appearance.

> Whereas you saw the feet and toes partly of potter's clay and partly of iron, the kingdom shall be divided.
>
> (v. 41)

This pattern of division is all the more remarkable as it comes after periods of unity.

The dream faithfully follows the fluctuations of history. After Rome, of which Pliny the Elder has said, "she had given Unity to the world,"[31] there will be no more unity. Only the nostalgia will remain, which will affect Charlemagne, Othon the Great, Napoleon, and Hitler, and which is still burning today in the hearts of the militants of a united Europe.

Secondly, the meaning of iron and clay concerns the parts which constitute the kingdom:

> And as the toes of the feet were partly of iron and partly of clay, so the kingdom shall be partly strong and partly fragile.
>
> (v. 42)

The emphasis here appears to be on the components of the kingdom, as if to suggest the cohabitation of two powers of different natures.

The iron, which refers to Rome, is then of a political nature and indicates, within this fifth kingdom, traces of the preceding power.

The clay, an unexpected material after the metals, indicates a power of an essentially different nature. In fact, the reference to the clay has a strong religious connotation which belongs to the biblical tradition.

In addition to the idea of fragility which is indicated in vv. 41, 42 to explain the reference to clay, this material also points to human creature; man of clay, Adam owes his existence to the intervention of the "potter" from above (Gen. 2:7; 3:19; Is. 64:8; Jer. 18:6ff.). Now, in the language of Daniel the reference to human creature conveys a specific religious connotation. Chapter 7, for example, brings out a human-featured little horn to represent a religious power, in opposition to the four animals, which stand for political powers (Daniel 7:8, 25. See our treatment of these passages below). Thus, Daniel evokes a religous power which, because of its fragility, needs to compromise with politics in order to insure its future.

In a third stage, iron and clay are interpreted as a mixture, and the meaning of "alliance" is deduced.

> As you saw iron mixed with ceramic clay, they will mingle with the seed of men; but they will not adhere to one another, just as iron does not mix with clay.
>
> (v. 43)

This latter meaning is momentous, for it is the only one that is explicitly situated in the time of the end, a time which will coincide with the coming of the kingdom of God.

> In the days of these kings, the God of heaven will set up a kingdom.
>
> (v. 44)

As a prelude to the heavenly kingdom, the time of the end appears to the prophet's eyes as a period of restless agitation when the leaders on earth are endeavoring to contract alliances which never materialize.

In summary, the prophet situates the time of the end:

1. In time, it occurs *after* the period which follows Rome, and *before* the end; it is therefore our present time.

2. In essence, the time of the end features a move toward alliances and appeals for unity.

It is still difficult to fully comprehend the scope of the vision. Whether it concerns the precise time of this period or the events which make up this period, the information remains vague. The scope is too wide.

The Rise of Beasts

Twice in a row the prophet is assailed by visions of animals which rise from the water and bring the march of history. First in chapter 7, they come as a nightmare: the prophet's spirit is beset by four strange beasts in the middle of the night. Then in chapter 8, the vision seems tamer and more acceptable to the "jewish" sensibility of the prophet. The animals which come up—a ram and a goat—are closer to his world.

Four Strange Beasts (Daniel 7)

Four Kingdoms

From the very first words, the language sounds familiar to Daniel. The beginning of the vision is an echo of the beginning of the Creation story in Gen. 1.[32] Here, as there, there is the presence of water and wind, and the wide scope of the universe, "the four winds of heaven."[33] From the start the evocation is suggestive enough to hint at the hidden lesson of the vision. The prophet immediately realizes that the whole universe is involved in a merciless struggle between the God on high, master of Creation, and the powers of darkness represented by tumultuous waters (cf. Is. 8:7ff.; Jer. 46:7, 9; 47:2; Rev. 17:1, 15).

A closer look reveals that the four beasts, which march onto the scene of history and represent universal kingdoms, are nothing but a broader and more precise restating of the data in chapter 2. In both passages, the symbols—animals and metals—

represent kingdoms. Both passages deal with four kingdoms. Both passages cover a period which leads to the end of time. This threefold coincidence allows for easy identification. The first beast, the lion, corresponds to the first kingdom of the statue, namely Babylon. The second beast, the bear, corresponds to the second kingdom, that of the Medes and Persians.[34] The third beast, the leopard, corresponds to the Greek Empire. Lastly, the fourth beast, dreadful with its iron teeth, corresponds to the fourth kingdom of the statue, Rome. Parallel to the fourth kingdom of the statue, the fourth beast likewise exerts its influence beyond its own time.

Ten Kingdoms

The fourth beast is described as having ten horns which represent a division into ten kingdoms (7:7b; 24a); it reminds of and parallels the division which takes place according to Daniel 2 after the fourth kingdom, Rome, and is also symbolically embodied in the ten toes. The use of ten here is noteworthy for two reasons. First, this is the number which, in biblical symbolism, conveys the idea of minimum,[35] or rather, as in the dialogue between God and Abraham (cf. Gen. 18:32), the number marking the boundary beyond which it is not appropriate to discuss. The division into ten kingdoms indicates a division beyond which one cannot go. The Roman Empire is parceled out to the utmost. The mention of ten kingdoms rising from the Roman Empire indicates the importance of the division, all the more remarkable as it comes after a period of strong unity. Secondly, one also recognizes, beyond this symbolic reference, a reference to some historic reality. From the ruins of the Roman Empire ten kingdoms or so were created.

At this point, we shall not go into details to disclose the exact identity of every one of these kingdoms.[36] One thing remains certain; after Rome there will be a great division.

A Different Power

Then, the prophecy continues. Arising in the midst of these kingdoms (v. 8), yet after them (v. 24b), is a strange and puzzling little horn which surprises the prophet to such an extent that he devotes the longest passage to it, thereby calling our attention to it. The first words tell us that this power is different in essence. "And another shall rise after them; he shall be different from the first ones" (7:24).

In fact, the little horn is singled out because it contains human features. It has human eyes and a talking mouth (7:8). In Daniel's language, the reference to human nature conveys a religious connotation (4:16; 7:4).[37] One remembers that on the statue of Daniel 2, the extension of the fourth kingdom also brought out clay, a material of a different nature. As we have already noted, this material portrays not only the religious character of the power, but also its ability to adapt to politics. Clay, the substance of man in Daniel 2, and the little horn, with its human features in Daniel 7, would then represent the same ambiguous power that is both religious and political. Indeed, this is the portrait drawn by the vision as it describes the little horn's activities: the little horn works on both levels, political and religious.

It is on a political level that this power shows itself in the first stage. "He shall subdue three kings" (7:24b; cf. 8:20). In another passage, the fall of these three kings (about one third of the whole) is directly attributed to the rise of the little horn (7:8, 20). The biblical notion of the "third," is commonly used in a perspective of destruction or of total victory.[38] Therefore it is directly linked with the rise of the little horn (7:8, 20). The fall of the three kings is brought about by the establishment of the little horn, setting the stage for what follows.

In the next phase, therefore, the little horn, which now has a great deal of elbow-room, extends its action to the religious level. Its religious activity relies on the political one and reflects the same aggressive behavior.

On the religious level the little horn works against God and his saints, as the alternate parallelism suggests:

A "He shall speak pompous words against the Most High" (against God)

B "Shall persecute the saints of the Most High" (against the saints)

C "And shall intend to change times and law" (against God)

D "And the saints shall be given into his hand for a time and times and half a time" (Daniel 7:25)[39]

This literary game conveys two lessons. 1) It shows a connection between the world of God in heaven and the world of the saints on the earth. 2) It indicates a complementary relationship between A and C above on one hand, and B and D on the other. A is complemented by C with regard to God, and likewise B is complemented by D with regard to the saints.

With regard to God, the little horn does not confine itself to presumptuous words against the Most High (v. 8), it also wants "to change times and law." In Daniel's language, this implies an attempt at usurping God, for to Daniel, only God can change the times (cf. Daniel 2:21). Actually the Bible explains this prerogative of God on the basis that, as the Creator, He is the only one who can control time (cf. Jer. 31:35; cf. Gen. 1:4, 14). By saying that the little horn would change times and law, Daniel may well then point to the law, which is, through the memory of Creation it conveys, the very sign of God's control on time, through the law of the Sabbath (Ex. 20:8-11). Moreover, the association "time-law" is also significant in this connection since it alludes to the Sabbath, a law which brings a dimension of time into the life of worship (see note 123). As a matter of fact, this reference to the Sabbath is suggested by the preceding prophecy of Daniel 2. Clay, which in Daniel 7 is the little horn, represents a religious power trying to compromise with politics. Significantly, Daniel 2 formulates this compromise in connection with the nature of clay, that is, through a subtle hint to the biblical event of Creation (Is. 64:8).

The changing of the Sabbath pointed out in Daniel 7 and the compromise with politics expressed in Daniel 2 then are connected. The changing of the Sabbath will be brought about on the basis of a compromise with politics.

With regard to the saints, the little horn does not limit itself to a particular intervention. It will exert its oppression *historically* for "one time, and two times,[40] and half a time," that is, three times and a half. Several elements indicate that the word "time" (in Aramaic *'iddān*) which is used here must be understood in the sense of years:

1. In a previous vision, the same word "time" had already been interpreted by the prophet in the sense of years (4:16; cf. 4:23, 25).

2. The Hebrew equivalent of the expression "a time, times and half a time" is used in Daniel 12:7 in connection with periods of 1290 days and 1335 days which cover about the same time span (1260 days[41]). Besides, all three lead roughly to the same time of the end (vv. 7, 9, 11, 12).

3. This computation is supported in the book of Revelation (cf. 11:2, 3; 12:6, 14; 13:5) where the same span of time for the same event is expressed in months (42 months) and in days (1260 days).[42]

The Day of Judgment

Finally, in the last portion of this history, blended with it, looms an unexpected event, the judgment.

The judgment is an integral part of human history,[43] as the structure of our passage suggests:

The vision is divided into three sections, each introduced by the same stylistic expression, "I saw in my vision by night" (vv. 2, 7, 13). Furthermore, within each section the introductory interjection "behold" (*ᵃrû*) (vv. 2, 5, 6, 7, 8 [2 times], 13)[44] is used seven times to mark the chronological progression.

The judgment scene comes in the second section, introduced by the second occurrence of the expression "I saw in my vision by night" (v. 7). It is also governed by the "behold" which is related to the coming of the little horn (v. 8). This literary observation allows us to infer that the judgment scene belongs both to the historical time of the second section and to the scope of the little horn's activity. So the prophet embraces the *heavenly* event of judgment as well as the *earthly* scene of the evil practices of the little horn, both at the same time. This peculiarity highlights an idea that is dear to Daniel: human history is not cut off from heaven, but develops in close connection with it. The literary structure of chapter 7 reflects this very thought. Three times, we shift alternatively from prose to poetry and from poetry to prose, following the prophet's gaze as it looks to earth or to heaven.

vv. 2-8	on earth, in prose
9, 10	in heaven, in poetry
11, 12	on earth, in prose
13, 14	in heaven, in poetry
15-22	on earth, in prose
23-27	in heaven, in poetry

In that way, a bond of mysterious dependence is suggested between the destiny of the earthly world and "history" in heaven, thereby opening a perspective of hope for this world.

In the light of chapter 7, some new data have been added to that of chapter 2. As in chapter 2, chapter 7 locates the time of the end roughly in the period that comes after Rome. As in chapter 2, chapter 7 points to a religious power that comes immediately after the division of the Roman Empire. However, in the same range of view as this particular power, chapter 7 highlights a new element, the dramatic action of God's judgment in heaven.

Yet frustration arises due to the incomplete information which remains. The identity of the little horn is not clear. Even though we know it shows up after the division of the Roman Empire and although its oppressive power is indicated, we do not yet fully understand the expression "one time, two times and half a time" (v. 25). The data of chapter 7 concerning the little horn still remain indefinite and the language is often puzzling.

Neither do we quite understand the meaning of this judgment which belongs to the course of human history and precedes the coming of the Kingdom of God. Daniel himself is quite upset after receiving this vision. "As for me, Daniel, my thoughts greatly troubled me, and my countenance changed; but I kept the matter in my heart" (Daniel 7:28).

Two Familiar Animals (Daniel 8)

Two Kingdoms

The vision of chapter 8 shares a lot of common themes with chapter 7. We are alert to this connection from the first words. The prophet intentionally ties this vision to the preceding one.

> A vision appeared to me—to me, Daniel—after the one that appeared to me the first time.
> (Daniel 8:1)

As in chapter 7, the succession of universal empires is told again by reference to animals. But here, for the first and only time in the book of Daniel, all the animals are explicitly identified. The ram is "the kings of Media and Persia" (Daniel 8:20) and the goat is "the kingdom of Greece" (Daniel 8:21). The four horns which arise from this animal out of a broken horn are "four kingdoms" (v. 22). The allusion of the prophecy is easy to detect. It is known that upon Alexander's death, the Greek empire was indeed divided into four kingdoms.

Then the prophetic word seems to rush along. Through a remarkable shortcut, the vision skips over the next link, the fourth kingdom, and comes to deal with "the little horn" (v. 9).

From the outset we may perceive at least two reasons why this link has been neglected in chapter 8:

1. Out of the experience of the previous vision of chapter 7, the prophet has developed a great concern regarding the little horn and is anxious to come back to it.
2. The fourth kingdom is the kingdom which received the most consideration in chapter 7 (Daniel 7:7, 8, 19, 23). It is, by the way, noteworthy that the ten horns are integrated in the fourth

kingdom (7:24). Although the ten kingdoms they represent will come afterward, the fourth beast is initially described as having ten horns. It is also significant that the paragraph dealing with the ten horns belongs to the same "behold" pattern as the fourth kingdom (7:7). This is not the case of the little horn which is introduced by a new "behold" (7:8) and belongs therefore to a section distinct from the fourth kingdom.

The fourth kingdom (the fourth beast with the ten horns) is thus "seen" by the prophet in its totality, i.e., in its time of unity as well as its period of divisions. The whole image is still vivid in Daniel's mind and therefore will be merely hinted at in the flow of the vision of Daniel 8.

A Different Power

The little horn which shows up in chapter 8 after the tumbling down of the universal kingdoms, resembles the appearance, activities and destiny of the little horn of chapter 7. In both chapters 7 and 8, the little horn comes at the same time, immediately after the universal empires (7:2-7, 15-20; cf. 8:2-8, 20-22). In chapter 7, as in chapter 8, the little horn stands in opposition to God, the saints and the law.

Against God, the little horn stands as a presumptuous and even usurpatory power in both chapters (7:25a; cf. 8:25b). Against the saints, the little horn exerts oppression and persecution in both chapters (7:25; cf. 8:24). Against the law, the little horn "shall intend to change times and law" (7:25), "cast truth down to the ground" (8:12). The word truth (*'emet*), which is used here, conveys the idea of faithfulness (from *'mn*) and is also an implicit reference to the law. The Scriptures often associate the Hebrew concept *'emet* (truth-faithfulness) and the concept of law (cf. Mal. 2:6; Ps. 119:43, 142, 151, etc.). The philosophical notion of truth is not part of the thought. Truth in Hebrew is that which stands in conformity to the law (cf. Mal. 2:6 and Rom. 2:20). Consequently, several Jewish commentators, including Ibn Ezra, Rashi, and Metsudath David, have perceived this passage (8:12) in the sense of a rejection of the law. "He (the little horn) will cancel the law (Torah) and the observance of the Ten Commandments."[45]

Finally, in both chapters, the little horn is related to a period of time: 1260 days in chapter 7, 2300 evenings and mornings in chapter 8.

Everything that happens to the little horn of chapter 7 has its counterpart in the little horn of chapter 8. Indeed, the little horn of chapter 8 and the little horn of chapter 7 are undoubtedly the same.

The Day of Atonement

The parallelism of motifs which relates the two chapters[46] goes beyond the epic of the little horn; it connects the judgment scene (ch. 7) and the cleansing of the sanctuary (ch. 8). The structure of the whole passage dealing with the little horn (8:9-14) likewise suggests the same up-and-down movement of the prophet's gaze between heaven and earth.

v. 9	And out of one of them came a little horn which grew exceedingly great toward the south, toward the east, and toward the glorious land—*earth*.
v. 10a	And it grew up to the host of heaven—*heaven*.
v. 10b	And it cast down some of the host and some of the stars to the ground, and trampled them—*earth*.
v. 11a	He even exalted himself as high as the Prince of the host—*heaven*.
vv.11b-12	And by him the daily sacrifices were taken away, and the place of His sanctuary was cast down. Because of transgression, an

army was given over to the horn to oppose the daily sacrifices; and he cast truth down to the ground. He did and all this and prospered—*earth*.

vv.13-14 Then I heard a holy one speaking; and another holy one said to that certain one who was speaking, "How long will the vision be, concerning the daily sacrifices and the transgression of desolation, the giving of both the sanctuary and the host to be trampled under foot?" And he said to him[47], "For two thousand three hundred days, then the sanctuary shall be cleansed"—*heaven*.

The last scene (vv. 13, 14), which deals with the cleansing of the sanctuary, is a dialogue between two heavenly beings and consequently belongs to the heavenly world,[48] thereby following the alternate movement of the prophet's gaze. Thus, the event of the cleansing of the sanctuary in chapter 8 as well as the event of the judgment in chapter 7 are seen in the same heavenly realm. Finally, both the cleansing of the sanctuary and the judgment belong to the same time of the end, the very time that precedes the coming of the heavenly kingdom (7:26; 8:17, 26).

The parallelism between the two chapters shows how related the judgment and the cleansing of the sanctuary are.[49] This particular connection is indeed suggestive to the Jewish mind, pointing to the Day of Atonement, the only day when the judgment is evoked and the sanctuary is cleansed.

Already, from the beginning of chapter 8, the imagery of the ram and the goat have paved the way for this reference to the Day of Atonement; the association of these two animals occurs precisely on that day (Lev. 16:5, 6).

Besides their function of representation in Daniel 8, the ram and the goat were then also designed to point to the Day of Atonement. Significantly, the biblical author resorts to several means to draw attention to the association of these two animals.

1. In the book of Daniel history regularly follows a cycle of four kingdoms[50] (ch. 2; 7; 11:1-4); only chapter 8 deals with two kingdoms. This breaking of the rules shows that the two animals are isolated on purpose.

2. The empires which were referred to through wild beasts (lion, bear, leopard, etc.) in chapter 7 are now, in chapter 8, unexpectedly represented by clean animals (the ram and the goat), which are familiar to the Israelites' way of life. The shift from unclean and wild animals to clean and familiar animals representing the same pagan empires betrays an obvious intention, to bring out the association of ram-goat, and to point to the Day of Atonement.

3. The four beasts of chapter 7, in contrast to the two animals of chapter 8, function as clear representatives of the empires they point to. Thus Babylon was traditionally represented by a lion, as attested to in the Bible and in archeology as well.[51] Even though the next beasts do not seem to be attested to in history as national symbols, they are described so as to correspond with their actions. The bear, which represents Persia, evokes the voracious conquests of the Persians.[52] The leopard, representing Greece, symbolizes the rapid[53] conquests of Greece; and if the leopard has four heads it is to suggest that its domination will extend to the whole earth, as conveyed through the symbolism of the number four.[54] Finally, the fourth beast "with huge iron teeth, devouring, breaking in pieces and trampling" embodies the totalitarian empire of Rome. The four beasts of Daniel 7 typify the empires they represent, whereas the two animals of Daniel 8 have nothing to do with the empires they are supposed to stand for. Consequently, if the motifs of the ram and the goat have been chosen to represent two empires while not resembling the characteristics of these empires, it is because they hold another function than just the illustrative one.

4. In Daniel 8, the prophet has omitted the two kingdoms which seem to be the most important to him, Babylon, the kingdom still present in Daniel's time (Daniel 2:38), and Rome, the strange and dreadful kingdom that fascinated him (Daniel 7:19). On the other hand the prophet has retained the two kingdoms which are comparatively insignificant (the Medes and Persians, and Greece). The intention of the biblical author is indicated here. If Daniel

has chosen these two kingdoms (the second and the third in the prophetic sequence of Daniel 2 and 7) rather than the other two in order to convey his message, it is precisely because of their insignificance. He wanted to focus attention *on the motif* of the ram and goat, rather than on the kingdoms themselves. What mattered to the prophet was not so much the two kingdoms *per se*, (Medes and Persians, and Greece), but the theme of the Day of Atonement.

We now understand why the little horn appears after Greece in Daniel 8, and not according to the sequence of Daniel 7, after Rome. The little horn is portrayed in Daniel 8 in a manner clear enough to suggest that it is the same little horn as in Daniel 7. Therefore, the mention of the kingdom which precedes the little horn (in Daniel 7, the fourth beast, i.e., Rome) is no longer required in Daniel 8. The expression "out of them" (8:9) should then be understood as related to the fourth beast of Daniel 7, which is implied in Daniel 8, and is not related to one of the horns of the third beast of Daniel 7, that is, Greece in Daniel 8. This is confirmed by the fact that the little horn is described as "coming out of the four winds of heaven" (8:8), a specific expression which is associated in Daniel 7 with the four beasts (7:2, 3). Also, this particular reference to the "winds of heaven" rather than to the four horns[55] may explain (or is confirmed by) the curious disagreement of genders in the Hebrew phrase "one (feminine) of them (masculine)" which parallels "winds (feminine) of heaven (masculine)."[56] This anomaly might have been intended as a literary device to suggest an organic link with the "winds of heaven" apart from the four horns mentioned just before.[57] Since the fourth beast is absent from Daniel 8, the author feels it necessary to refer to it by means of the general expression "one of them," i.e. one of the four winds of heaven, thereby implying the presence of all four beasts of Daniel 7. As a matter of fact, this interpretation is implied in the angel's explanation in 8:23. There, the advent of the little horn intervenes "far after (*'aḥ*ᵃ*rîṯ*) these kingdoms,"[58] and not immediately after them, which suggests that the little horn comes after the period of time which follows the third kingdom, hence after the fourth kingdom.

Undoubtedly this special concern to isolate and underline the association of the two animals (the ram and the goat) in order to convey a hint of the Day of Atonement was to prepare the ground for the follow-up. Indeed, in the extension of this passage, at the climax of the vision, there is a direct reference to the Day of Atonement. The prophet speaks in Daniel 8:14 of the cleansing of the sanctuary. It is significant that the obscure expression *niṣdaq*, which literally means "be reinstated in its rights,"[59] has been translated by the Septuagint as the "cleansing" (*katharisthesetai*) of the sanctuary. The scholars of the Septuagint had understood this passage as a reference to the Day of Atonement, the very day when the sanctuary was cleansed (Lev. 16:19, 30). It is also the same interpretation which Rashi himself supports as he reads into this verse a direct allusion to the atonement (*kpr*) of the sins of Israel.[60]

It is significant that among the connotations conveyed in the root *ṣdq* the one pointing to the Day of Atonement was retained. This option of the Septuagint and of the Jewish tradition, as attested in Rashi, is moreover illuminated and supported by Daniel 9:24. It relates *ṣdq* to the verb *kpr* (atonement) by means of the synonymous parallelism: "to make atonement (*kpr*) for iniquity, to bring everlasting righteousness (*ṣdq*)". One is therefore entitled to suggest on the basis of this observation that when Daniel uses the word *ṣdq* in 8:14, he has a process of atonement in mind.

Thus, in Daniel 8 the prophet beholds a Kippur in heaven. This is indicated by the way this event parallels the heavenly judgment of Daniel 7. It is found exactly at the corresponding point of the sequence:

Daniel 7	Daniel 8
animals for kingdoms (vv. 4-7)	animals for kingdoms (vv. 3-9a)
little horn (v. 8)	little horn (vv. 9b-13)

heavenly judgment (vv. 9-12) ⟷ Kippur (v. 14)

Kingdom of God (vv. 13-14) Kingdom of God (v. 25b)

As a matter of fact, every element of the drama of the Judgment is present in the ceremony of Kippur: the separation of the two goats (Lev. 16:8-10), the remembrance of all the sins of the past year (Lev. 16:34), the universal dimension of the atonement, which involves the entire people (Lev. 16:33), and the mandatory fasting (Lev. 16:29).

To this day, the Israelites celebrate Kippur as the symbol of the great Day of Judgment. To realize how strong this reference is, one must have experienced the unique atmosphere of this festival. Thoughts of the judgment beset and haunt the spirit of the Jew throughout Kippur. Clearly identifying these two events are the prayers which are recited, prayers which have been composed for this sacred time. Trembling with the joy and the fear of God, the man of Israel experiences Kippur, the Day of Judgment. According to old tradition, at Kippur, "God is seated on His throne to judge the world. Simultaneously the judge, pleader, expert, and witness, openeth the Book of Records, and it is read, everyman's signature being found therein. The great trumpet is sounded; a still, small voice is heard; the angels shudder, saying, this is the day of judgment. . . ."[61]

Kippur, the cleansing of the sanctuary, and the judgment are the same event. This identification allows us to locate the event on the prophetic calendar, for it is in connection with the cleansing of the sanctuary that, for the first time, a specific measure of time is indicated. The "two thousand three hundred evenings and mornings," while providing the time of the cleansing of the sanctuary, by the same clue also locate the time of judgment. Now, if we take the prophecy of Daniel at its word as pointing to real history, we can risk the adventure of research.

The problem stands in these terms: we are informed that a period of time, 2300 evenings and mornings, will elapse until the time of the end. Yet we have neither the starting point, nor the conversion key which would enable us to interpret the figure. In fact, the vision of chapter 8 limits the scope of its revelation.

The question of Daniel, who "seeks understanding" (*bîn*) regarding the vision of the 2300 evenings and mornings (v. 15), is answered by the angel Gabriel: "Understand (*bîn*), son of man, that the vision refers to the time of the end" (v. 17).

The repetition of the verb *bîn* (to understand) in the question and answer indicates the intention of the biblical author to limit, for the moment, the understanding (*bîn*) of Daniel to the fact that this vision refers to the time of the end only. Thus Daniel remains perplexed and frustrated and the chapter ends with the admission that he does not understand (*'ên meḇîn*, v. 27). The last note of chapter 8 is a negative one because of Daniel's need to understand the vision, and consequently with his expectation of a complement of information.[62]

A Prophetic Calendar

The prophet Daniel was left preoccupied with the vision of the 2300 evenings and mornings. What did this figure mean? What period of time did it cover? What was its starting point and its conclusion? What was the meaning of the event it pointed to, the reference to the judgment and the Day of Atonement? These questions were left unanswered.

Another prophecy will provide the prophet with the answer and the explanation he is looking for as it takes over the use of the verb "understand," which is the key theme of Daniel 8 (see vv. 5, 15, 16, 23, 27).[63] From precise "chronological milestones," a prophetic calendar will be unfolded within the course of history.

Chronological Milestones (Daniel 9)

The Thread

Ch. 8 ended on the "not understanding" (*bîn*). The thread of this very theme (*bîn*) is taken over immediately in the introduction of chapter 9; Daniel is said here to have understood (*bîn*) the seventy-years prophecy of Jeremiah. Now the tone is positive, as if what will be dealt with in Daniel 9 has to be placed in conjunction with Daniel 8, as its continuation, i.e. its answer.

The next time the verb "to understand" reappears is in v. 22, at the beginning of a new prophecy. A time of seventy weeks is determined until the coming of a Messiah, when violent death is foretold against the background of salvation and the atonement for sins.[64]

In this sentence, the angel Gabriel helps Daniel "understand" the prophecy of the seventy weeks. It echoes the words spoken by the same angel in Daniel 8:16 to offer "understanding" regarding the prophecy of the 2300 evenings and mornings.

> Make understand (*haḇen*) . . . the vision (8:16)
> Understand (*haḇen*) . . . the vision (9:23)

Actually, Daniel 8:16 contains the first occurrence of the form *haḇen* (to understand) and Daniel 9:23 has the last one, as if the thought of the key-word *haḇen*, started in Daniel 8:16, had finally reached its goal in Daniel 9:23. It is evident here that the prophecy of the 70 weeks was intended to be part of the preceding prophecy of 2300 evenings and mornings which had been left incomplete. Underlying this connection between the 70 weeks and the 2300 evenings and mornings is the word which introduces the prophecy of the 70 weeks, "cut off" (*ḥtk*). The fact that the 70 weeks of Daniel 9 are said to be "cut off" implies that they must belong to a longer and already known period of time, i.e. the 2300 evenings and mornings of Daniel 8.[65]

The first revelation provides the information about the duration of the period, 2300 evenings and mornings, which leads to the "time of the end" (8:17). The second revelation provides the complementary data, the starting point of this period.

The Starting Point

In fact, the prophecy of Daniel 9 gives the period of the 70 weeks a precise starting point, which is therefore the starting point of the related 2300 evenings and mornings as well.

From the going forth of the command
To restore and build Jerusalem
Until Messiah the Prince,
There shall be seven weeks and sixty-two weeks . . .
And after the sixty-two weeks,
Messiah shall be cut off . . . .
(Daniel 9:25,26)

It is, then, a decree, the order to rebuild Jerusalem, which is used as a springboard for the prophecy. We learn from the book of Ezra that the city of Jerusalem and its temple were indeed rebuilt upon publication of three successive decrees issued by Cyrus, Darius, and Artaxerxes respectively (Ezra 6:14).

Several clues point to the decree of Artaxerxes: this is the last one and consequently the only one to be effective. This is also the only complete one; it concerns the building of the temple as well as restoring the administrative and political role of the city of Jerusalem. It is, moreover, the only one which is followed by a blessing and praise to God, and indeed the only one which refers to God's intervention.

> Blessed be the Lord God of our fathers, who has put such a thing as this in the king's
> heart to beautify the house of the Lord which
> is in Jerusalem.
> (Ezra 7:27)

It is also significant that from this blessing and praise—Ezra's reaction to the action of God—the text passes from the Aramaic language to the Hebrew language. The decree of Artaxerxes generated this shift, suggesting that the national restoration commenced here.[66]

Artaxerxes issued this decree in the seventh year of his reign, that is in the autumn of 457 B.C.[67] The year 457 B.C. is, then, the starting point of the 2300 evenings and mornings as well as of the 70 weeks.

The Conversion Key

That the 70 weeks have to be interpreted in terms of years is evidenced by the biblical text itself:

1. Following the Hebrew literary device of composition, the introduction (vv. 1-4) and the conclusion (vv. 20-27) echo each other in terms of the same inquiry (computation of times) and the same number (70). Thus the bridge between the 70 years of the introduction of Daniel 9 and the 70 weeks of its conclusion helps to decipher the word "weeks." The two expressions, *šiḇʿîm šānāh* in v. 2 and *šāḇuʿîm šiḇʿîm* in v. 24, point to each other by the means of the following chiasmus:

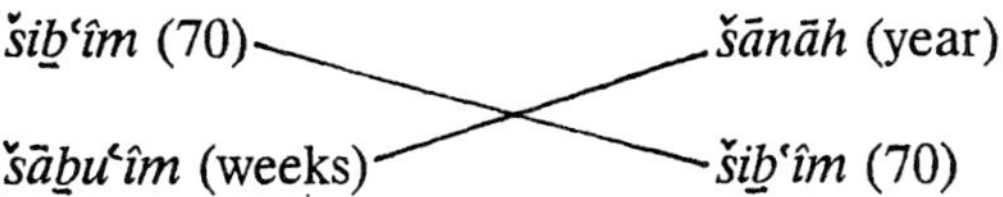

This chiasmus elucidates the nature of the weeks; as *šiḇʿîm* is equivalent to *šiḇʿîm*, so *šāḇuʿîm* is equivalent to *šānāh*. From the outset, the text of Daniel 9 indicates, in an allusive manner, the nature of these weeks to be read as years.

2. Immediately following chapter 9, in the initial verses of chapter 10, Daniel suggests the meaning of "weeks." Referring to his three weeks of fasting, Daniel specifies in Hebrew "weeks of days" (v. 2). This is the only passage in the whole Bible to use such an expression in order to distinguish the two kinds of weeks. As an author puts it, "The expression 'three full weeks' means literally 'three weeks of days' and is probably used to differentiate from the phrase 'weeks of years' that is clearly implied in Dan. 9."[68] The three weeks of fasting are made up of days, whereas the 70 weeks are made up of years.

Outside of the book of Daniel, the book of Ezekiel and others substantiate the same equation: one day equals one year (see Ez. 4:4-7). Furthermore, Jewish tradition has always understood the seventy weeks in this way,[69] and this interpretation is attested as far back as the second century B.C. in Qumran.[70] To conclude, using the conversion key of one day equaling one year, the 70 weeks of Daniel 9 would therefore lead us from 457 B.C. precisely to the year 31 A.D., the date of Christ's death.[71]

Since the prophecy of 70 weeks and the prophecy of 2300 evenings and mornings belong to the same chronological line as if in perspective, then the same conversion key—one day equals one year—must apply to the latter prophecy as well.

Before we consider the implications of the interpretation of the 2300 evenings and mornings, we may incidentally notice that the conversion key for the period of the 1260 days (a time, times, a half time) is likewise provided by this understanding of the 70 weeks relating to the 2300 days. This period of time corresponds with the parallel prophecy of chapter 7. The 1260 days as well as the 2300 days must therefore be understood in the sense of years.

This connection between the 1260 days-years and the 2300 evenings and mornings must not, however, lead us astray. In this instance it is merely a parallelism of motifs. The correspondence of motifs does not necessarily mean an equivalence in terms of the duration and of the event it implies. The data are explicit enough to suggest two different periods:

1. The 1260 days indicate a duration—the length of time of the oppression of the little horn: "the saints shall be given into his hand *for* a time and times and half a time" (Daniel 7:25). The 2300 evenings and mornings indicate a date. This is the moment when the process of the cleansing of the sanctuary starts: "for 2300 evenings and mornings, *then* the sanctuary shall be cleansed" (Daniel 8:14).

2. The 1260 days begin as soon as the little horn is well settled, after the division of Rome (Daniel 7:24). The 2300 evenings and mornings, seen *in the perspective of* the 70 weeks, start at the same time as the 70 weeks, 457 B.C.

3. The 1260 days end somewhere before the time of judgment and are distinct from it (7:25, 26) since they are not supposed to direct to it. The 2300 evenings and mornings end precisely at the Day of Atonement since they are designed to point to it.

These essential differences relative to the functions of the two times will subsequently affect the way they are situated. The 1260 days are inserted in a span of time with no indication as to when they will start or end, as if this specification was insignificant. After all, the prophet is not so much concerned with the exact moment the oppression begins, as with its duration—that is, not "when?" but "how long?" In contrast, the vision of the 2300 evenings and mornings is more precise, and all the information delineating it is provided. This vision does have starting and ending points.

The Termination

Put in the same perspective as the 70 weeks, the 2300 evenings and mornings transport us from 457 B.C. to the heart of the 19th century, more precisely, to 1844.

This precision is surprising and even disturbing. As long as the prophecy remains nebulous, abstract, symbolical, and distant, we can follow it and even enjoy it. But as soon as the prophet's vision happens to become specific and has the impudence to concern our modern times, then it becomes paradoxically suspect.

How can it be that God would have spoken so far into the future, and that God could still be present in our enlightened and secular times? If we believe Daniel, 1844 has its place in the prophetic calendar just as surely as the year 31.

Theological Application

The fact that the events of the years 31 and 1844 are related conveys a theological meaning too, we shall examine in the rest of this chapter.

The Levitical Ritual

The sanctuary and its services are explicitly referred to in both prophecies; and this Levitical preoccupation shines through the language. It is significant indeed that the key verbs in both events are all in the *Niphal* form, which happens to be a technical form of the priestly "declaratory verdict."[72] Daniel 9 describes the action by the use of 6 verbs: determined (v. 24), shall be built (v. 25), shall be cut off (v. 26), determined (v. 26), determined (v. 27), poured out (v. 27). Daniel 8 uses only one verb, "shall be cleansed" (v. 14). This 6 + 1 = 7 occurrence may convey a rhetorical device to suggest, again, the complementary connection between the two prophecies. The very Levitical texture in which both prophecies are woven not only substantiates their chronological connection, but also points in depth to the theological meaning of this connection.

Within the text regarding the atonement, the two prophecies meet in the common theme of the High Priest. Daniel 9:24 and Ex. 29:36, 37 are the only biblical passages using the association of three specific motifs, namely atonement, anointing, and Most Holy. This echo intimates a bridge between the two texts. As Daniel wrote 9:24, he must have had Ex. 29:36, 37 in mind.

In context, Ex. 29:36, 37 deals with the ordination of the first High Priest in Israel and refers to the institution of the "continual burnt offering," a token of God's presence among His people.

> This shall be a continual burnt offering throughout your generations at the door of the tabernacle of meeting before the Lord, where *I will meet* you to speak with you. And there *I will meet* with the children of Israel, and the tabernacle shall be sanctified by my glory.
>
> (Ex. 29:42-44)

By echoing the text of Exodus 29, the prophecy of Daniel 9 directly connects the event of the atoning death of the Messiah with the ordination of the High Priest and the institution of the sign of the permanent presence of God among His people, namely the continual burnt offering.

On the other hand, the prophecy of 2300 evenings and mornings implies the involvement of the High Priest as it relates to the Day of Atonement. Indeed, the reference to the High Priest is repetitively connoted in the word Prince (*śār*). This word (*śār*) points to the High Priest in many texts of the Old Testament

(1 Chron. 15:22; 24:5; Ezra 8:24). Within the book of Daniel, *śār* refers to Michael (10:5, 13, 21; 12:1), whose garments of linen are reminiscent of the Day of Atonement, the only day the priest was thus dressed (Lev. 16:4).[73]

The description of this heavenly personage in Daniel 10 strongly resembles that of the extraordinary figure in Ezekiel (Ez. 1:26-28).[74] Involving a heavenly personage, the ceremony which develops here has a very specific setting; it is a Kippur which takes place in heaven.

In summary, the study of the prophecy of Daniel 8 and its connection with Daniel 9 brings out two basic observations. The first observation is that Daniel not only implicitly, but explicitly refers to the Day of Atonement. Let us review the arguments leading to this conclusion.

1. The Septuagint version has preserved a translation of Daniel 8:14 which points to the cleansing of the sanctuary—that is, the Day of Atonement, thereby supporting an old tradition of interpretation which was later adopted by Rashi.

2. The parallelism between the sequence of the events reported in Daniel 7 and that of Daniel 8 makes the judgment and the Day of Atonement coincide. This correspondence is also confirmed outside Daniel, by the liturgical and rabbinical Jewish tradition which relates the Day of Atonement to the Day of Judgment.

3. The unexpected use of the association of ram-goat in Daniel 8 alludes to the Levitical ritual of Kippur.

4. The designation of the *śār* (prince) as the main personage involved there and His clothes of linen hint at the High Priest at work on the Day of Atonement.

The second observation concerns the theological lesson conveyed in the connection between the two predicted events. On one hand, the prophecy of 70 weeks foretells the coming of a Messiah by reference to the first ordination of the High Priest and his role in the continual offering. On the other hand, the prophecy of 2300 evenings and mornings foretells the coming of Kippur by reference to the princely figure of the High Priest in service on the Day of Atonement. The two events are set up in connection with each other, and are placed in the same perspective, pointing in the same direction—to salvation. Obviously this is the kind of connection which may have inspired Heb. 9:11-14, where the cross and the Day of Atonement are indeed seen in the same perspective and therefore seem to be identified in the text.[75]

How then can we avoid thinking of the Levitical ritual which pulsated in the Israelite's life?

Throughout the year, the "continual burning" occupied the altar (Num. 28:3). The Israelite always had to renew his sacrifices in order to ensure the atonement of his sins. The way this ceremony was conducted was significant in this respect.

The Israelite brought his offering, extended his hand over the head of the victim and confessed his sin, thus transferring it to the victim. He slaughtered the animal himself. The priest then took the blood into the sanctuary (only the first compartment, the Holy Place; Heb. 9:6; Lev. 4:6). Thus, the blood of the animals which figuratively carried the sin was transmitted to the sanctuary, a sign of the incarnated presence of God (Ex. 25:8).

But this was not enough. The stain under the tent remained foul and gory all year. Apparently the confessed sin, with its weight of death, had not departed from the tent to reach the heavenly mercy. One had to wait until the Day of Atonement to make sure that "all the iniquities" (Lev. 16:29, 34) were finally forgiven, rubbed out, atoned for, as implied in the meaning of the word Kippur.[76]

This was a unique occasion. For the first time the High Priest could enter the second compartment—the Holy of Holies. The blood was then sprinkled on the Mercy-seat under which were preserved the tables of the law (Deut. 10:5; cf. Ex. 26:34; Heb. 9:4). Then as a last step, the sins were finally transferred to the "goat for Azazel," a personification of evil,[77] which was chased into the wilderness. All the sins compressed under the tent were freed, pulverized into the vacuum of the wilderness. Then the sanctuary was declared "cleansed" (Lev. 16:16, 19).

The prophetic sketch bridging the years 31 and 1844 in the vision of Daniel 8 and 9 can be recognized here. These two dates are situated in time in such a way as to suggest a different function in the prophetic calendar. The first date, 31, indicates the precise moment of the death of the Messiah. "After the sixty-two weeks Messiah shall be cut off" (Daniel 9:26). The second date, 1844, indicates the end of a period, answering the question of one of the angels: "How long will the vision be, concerning the daily sacrifice? . . . And he said to me, for two thousand three hundred days . . ." (Daniel 8:13a, 14a). The 70-weeks prophecy gives the date of an event; the 2300-evenings-and-mornings prophecy gives a period of time at the end of which an event will occur, "then the sanctuary shall be cleansed" (Daniel 8:14b). In other words, the first dating (Daniel 9) is punctual and directly concerns the event it predicts, the death of the Messiah. The second dating (Daniel 8) is, so to speak, "open," and points to an event which starts in 1844 and goes beyond. This different way of dealing with the two times is paralleled in the two verbs which express the respective actions of the two events. The death of the Messiah is indicated by means of the imperfect (*yikkaret*: he shall be cut off), a tense which conveys the dynamics of a definite action.[78] The cleansing of the sanctuary is signified by means of the *perfectum propheticum*, a tense which points to the nature of the fact per se[79] (*w^enişdaq*: the cleansing will be operated). The death of the Messiah occurs in 31 and is confined to this date, whereas the cleansing of the sanctuary goes beyond the year 1844 and covers a time which Daniel describes as being "the time of the end" (cf. Daniel 8:17, 26). The two events are, to be sure, related, yet they hold different functions in the plan of salvation.

Two Phases of Salvation

Just as the Day of Atonement complements the "continual burning," so the event started in 1844 complements the drama perpetrated in 31. According to the Levitical ritual and the two prophecies of Daniel, salvation would not then be achieved instantly.

The history of heaven's intervention is imprinted by two dramas. It is in two steps that man is wrenched from the oppression of evil and death. The first weighs on the human conscience. It is the "lamb of God who takes away the sin of the world" (John 1:29). It is God's sacrifice in the human flesh. The second is beyond human consciousness. It is the heavenly process of God's definitive forgiveness.

So if God's earthly operation of *the historical act of rescue* has been fulfilled and there is nothing more to add, there is still the *decision of salvation* to be made in heaven on the Day of Atonement. Only then are the books opened (Daniel 7:10); only then does God ratify the earthly sacrifice so that the atonement may be achieved.

The event of judgment is expected, not in fear and anguish or as a terrible sentence, but as the ultimate point of hope. Indeed, judgment is essentially atonement rather than condemnation and belongs to the salvation process. This is implicitly indicated in the mention of the "open books" (Daniel 7:10) which are always associated in the Bible with saved people (Ex. 32:32; Ps. 56:8; 69:28; 139:16; Mal. 3:16; Daniel 7:10; 12:1-3). This is explicitly said by Daniel himself: "Judgment was made in favor of the saints" (Daniel 7:22).

So the judgment which opened in 1844 carries the same concern for salvation as the event which took place in 31. The two events belong to the same plan and necessarily complement each other on every level.

Love and Justice

On God's level, the incredible act of the cross, the incarnation of the love of heaven, also appeals to the concept of justice. It could not be otherwise. In Hebrew love is justice. The same root, *ṣdq*,[80] conveys both notions which are disassociated in our languages. In the Bible, it is inconceivable to separate love from justice; therefore, the two are identified together.

So, the sacrifice of Christ was not enough to resolve the problem. Salvation had to be mixed with judgment. Salvation had to be achieved according to the criterion of justice. Love had to be demonstrated, not as an arbitrary act, but as an intelligent operation "justifiable" in the eyes of the whole universe.

Through judgment, God accounts for His act of salvation. "The books are open;" proven evidence is shown that God's salvation is just and right.

Grace and Law

On man's level, the consciousness of having received grace from above explodes into the choice for a new life, henceforth tuned to the will of heaven.

Love does not exclude justice. When saved by God, one cannot help living according to God. Indeed, God saves the sinner, but only the sinner who repents. The one who does not repent does not know (and is unaware) that he is a sinner.

Salvation is complete. The cross implies the faith of the believer who accepts God's salvation (Eph. 1:13). Judgment implies the obedience of the believer who decides to live according to God's law. Both inside and outside, subjectively and objectively, man is saved.

The salvation of the cross must wait for the sifting of judgment. Therefore it is impossible to stand in the perspective of the cross without standing in the perspective of the judgment.

The Cross and the Waiting for the Kingdom

In the plan of salvation, the event of the cross brings along the waiting for the kingdom at the time of judgment. If God consented to the cross, it was not merely to demonstrate the quality of His love for man. God suffered the cross to offer man the chance to belong to His kingdom. The event of the cross is meaningful only in connection with the kingdom above.

Therefore it was inevitable that the event of salvation would be articulated in two steps. First is the cross, the act of God's incarnation and sacrifice; the second, at the end of human history, the waiting time, is the act of the judgment or Kippur, which prepares both heaven and earth for the heavenly kingdom.

The Reality of the Event

In historical reality, the judgment weighs as heavily and determining as the event of incarnation and the cross. If the drama predicted by the 70-weeks prophecy is part of history, then that of the 2300 evenings and mornings should share in the same treatment.

One may wonder about the nature of this event which is taking place in heaven, which the Bible describes with the strange term of Kippur. Does this mean that there, as in the ancient city of Israel, a tent is pitched, with a roof and curtains, and that in 1844 a personage vested with the function of High Priest passed from one compartment to another as prescribed in the Levitical system (cf. Lev. 16:2)? This scene is difficult to imagine because it seems to point to a theatrical performance rather than to the activity of a God dealing with man's salvation. This sounds awkward and against the familiar idea of a God who is beyond space and time.

But, in spite of our uneasiness and philosophical presuppositions, we must admit that God may very well have played this game, and that the irrationality of a fact does not challenge the reality of that fact. We must also notice that the Bible has accustomed us to these incursions of God into time and space. The God of the Bible is not the God of the philosophers, an abstraction, a principle; He is a person in history who acts, intervenes and surprises—a living Being. He is a historical God, so historical that He entered human history by becoming flesh, giving Himself over to the agony of the cross. The God of the Bible is a God who exists —to the point that we can dare to say He is a God who exists somewhere, in a place that is precisely located in space.

> "Look down from your holy inhabitation, from heaven."
>
> Deut. 26:15

> "Who is like the Lord our God who dwells on high. . . ."
>
> Ps. 113:5

> "In my Father's house are many mansions. . . ."
>
> John 14:2

A heavenly temple with two compartments and a Day of Atonement taking place there at a given time in human history should not repel us. This is after all possible, for the geography and the works of heaven will always be far beyond what we can see, understand or imagine. One thing is sure, however. God is to us what He gives of Himself, what He reveals of Himself. The point is not what is really occurring in His world. The point is not, how did the event of 1844 happen in heaven? The point is that we can only comprehend it through reference to something which belongs to our world, in this instance the Jewish Kippur. We must be content with it assuming, against our human reasoning, that it has the same reality as the death of Christ. No matter how it happens, the fact is, it does happen.

* * * *

In summary, the connection between the two events of salvation, respectively predicted in the 70-weeks prophecy, and in the 2300-evenings-and-mornings prophecy, conveys several truths:

1. It enables us to set up the chronology of the prophecies and indicates the starting point of those periods.
2. It confirms the sketch of the Levitical ritual.
3. It indicates that the act of rescue at the cross is made effective through the decision of salvation on the day of judgment.
4. It reveals the quality of God's love which also relates to the requirement of justice.
5. It demonstrates the blossoming of grace in a life open to the law of heaven.
6. It relates the event of the cross to the anticipation of the kingdom.
7. It shows that the event of the judgment has the same reality as the event of the cross.

Therefore the Time of Judgment conveys hope and becomes essentially a Time of Waiting for the believer.

CHAPTER TWO

A VISION OF WAITING

"Blessed is he who waits."

Daniel 12:12

The book of Daniel is imbued with the tensions of waiting. Daniel wrote against the background of exile. His book starts with the exile and all his stories and visions take place there. Daniel and his people are waiting for the restoration. This is explicitly stated in Daniel's prayer in chapter 9, the only prayer pronounced in the book, the only passage where Daniel is concerned with the actual destiny of his people. The prayer stems from the consultation contained in the "books" in which restoration is outlined. It starts with the prophecy of Jeremiah (Daniel 9:2); then it develops into a long plea for forgiveness, and finally closes with a pathetic cry: "do not delay!" (9:19). The whole prayer was directed towards this theme of waiting.

Daniel's "impatience" for the descent of God pervades his own experiences. The first ten days spent in Babylon are days of tense waiting. Daniel and his companions wait for the result of their act of faith and for a miracle from God. The expression "at the end of the days" (1:18), which is associated with the result, at the same time reveals the passion of waiting. The last verse of chapter 1 concludes by suggesting the same disposition of waiting: "thus Daniel continued until . . ." (1:21).

Chapters 3, 4, 5 and 6 bring out this motif by opposing the non-waiting mentality of the pagan king to the waiting attitude of the Hebrews. In chapter 3, the king wants the everlasting kingdom *now*. As a response to his dream warning him that he was going to be only the head of gold (2:38-40), implying an end to his kingdom, Nebuchadnezzar makes a whole statue of gold (3:1). In chapter 4 Nebuchadnezzar is again concerned with the Babylon of "today," enjoying the kingdom of the present (4:30). Similarly in chapter 5, Belshazzar is only interested in the present, engaging in revelry praising the visible gods which provide immediate satisfaction (5:4, 23).

On the other hand, while the king refers to the present and immediate condition, "if you do not worship, you shall be cast *immediately*" (3:15), the Hebrews refer to the future. "Our God will deliver us from your hand" (3:17), and they even dare to point to the far future beyond their present existence, "but if not . . ." (3:18). In the same way chapter 6 tells us about Daniel's reaction to the threatening king's decree (6:7). Daniel at once went home and opened his windows toward Jerusalem. His prayer is not so much concerned with the holy place, geographically speaking, as it is with his longing to return there. This look to Jerusalem should not be interpreted in terms of space, but in terms of time. Daniel wants and hopes for a better time of free worship. Furthermore, he goes beyond the mere waiting; as the text says, he keeps waiting, he prays three times that day "as was his custom since early days" (6:10). Daniel is "patiently patient."

Significantly, this ability to wait is described in the book of Daniel as the very virtue of wisdom insofar as wisdom is related to the *time* of waiting. In chapter 1 the amount of wisdom imparted to Daniel and his companions is in proportion to the number of days of waiting: ten times wiser—ten days (1:20). Chapters 2 and 7 associate wisdom with the idea of changing times (2:20-21) and of "after;" in these chapters we learn that there is always an "after." Kingdoms always have an "after them" (2:29, 39, 45; 7:5, 6, 7, 8, 24). Wisdom is precisely that ability to manage with time, that is, to see through time, and to know that there is an "after" (2:21-23, 45, 47). In this sense, Daniel is a wise man[81] (2:18, 19, 29-30, etc.).

Thus, we can understand why "those who are wise" in 12:3 applies to a people who are compared to a woman in labor (12:1). The expression "time of trouble" is a reminiscence of the texts of Jeremiah (30:6, 7; cf. 49:24; 50:43) which use it within the conjugal terminology of pregnancy to refer to the final salvation[82] (cf. Matt. 24:21, John 16:21). In Daniel 12:1 this sense is obvious since the "time of trouble" leads to the deliverance of birth, *mlṭ* (12:1b), a term which also belongs to the same metaphor (cf. Ps. 22:6; Prov. 11:21; Job 22:30).

If we read our text in the light of the passages of Jeremiah, this "waiting" takes on a particular perspective. Jeremiah compares the eschatological waiting to the "trouble of Jacob" (Jer. 30:7), thereby pointing to Gen. 32:7 which uses the same words. To the latter connection there is a related cluster of associations which fit perfectly in the context of Daniel 12:3. The threat of Edom the brother is hinted at here, a reminder of the great conflict against the traditional enemy and oppressor of Israel, Amalek (cf. Gen. 36:12; Ex. 17:16; Deut. 25:17-19; cf. the book of Obadiah; cf. Est. 3:1). Also the anguish of Jacob is evoked when he is confronted at night with a future he cannot anticipate; and beyond this experience of hopelessness (Gen. 32:11, 24, 26), there is the hopeful prospect of the country of Canaan. To be wise means, then, to be able to see beyond the thick cloud of God's silence, hoping for the kingdom; it means to be able to wait, because one knows that there is an "after."

Accordingly, it is no wonder that Daniel describes the time of the end as a Day of Atonement, a festival which was experienced in Israel as a time of intense hope and waiting. The *De Profundis* Psalm (Ps. 130), which draws its inspiration from the Day of Atonement[83] witnesses these feelings of hope and waiting.[84]

I wait for the Lord, my soul waits,
And in His word I do hope.
My soul waits for the Lord
More than those who watch for the morning—
I say, more than those who watch for the morning.
O Israel, hope in the Lord. . . .
(Ps. 130:5-7)

Actually, the whole prophecy of Daniel tends towards this "waiting," and it is not fortuitous that the book should end on the note: "Blessed is he who waits and comes to the 1335 days" (Daniel 12:12). The waiting hinted at here goes beyond mere expectation since it is paired with happiness. Moreover, the Hebrew verb *ḥkh*, for waiting, conveys a yearning for the best, a hope,[85] which characterizes those who will reach this time.

It is also noteworthy that the period of 1335 days is the last time period to be mentioned. It is also the only one to be marked by the feeling of arrival, after the waiting tension implied in the question "how long?" (Daniel 12:6).

The text provides an additional clue which confirms this connection between Daniel 12:6 and Daniel 8. Both prophecies are an answer to the same question "how long?" (*'aḏ-māṯay,* literally: until when? [Daniel 12:6; Daniel 8:13]). Both are associated with the same motif of "wonders" (Daniel 8:13, 24; 12:6) and within the same context of dialogue setting (Daniel 8:13; 12:6). This identical language indicates the same concern; both visions point to the same time. Therefore, the 1335 days, like the 2300 evenings and mornings, should end at 1844.

Thus, Daniel not only foretold 1844 through the 2300 evenings and mornings, but he also perceived this time from another vantage point, after 1335 days. In the prophecy of the 2300 evenings and mornings he looks up into heaven, to take in the scene of judgment.

In the prophecy of the 1335 days, he looks down on earth, to catch the happiness of waiting.

On the level of the believer, the time of the end could only be a time of happy waiting because it is the time in which he prepares for the kingdom of God. Yet, this waiting is not confined to passive happiness. Because it is the time of the end it also proves to be a time of denunciation and of proclamation; people on the earth have to be warned, and consequently urged to a better preparation.

The Denunciation

The time of the end is the time when the little horn is finally unmasked. Being a time of waiting, it is a time when the claims of the little horn and its identity are to be unveiled. Here, the preparation necessarily implies the difficult task of denunciation. To be well equipped in the perspective of the kingdom it is also important to be warned. The data are already sufficient to infer at least that the little horn cannot be Antiochus Epiphanes as alleged by the critics:

1. Its time: the little horn appears *after* the fourth kingdom, more precisely after all the universal kingdoms, and after the 3rd century A.D. Moreover, its activity extends until the end of the times.

2. Its activities: the little horn directs its attacks against the people of God through persecution and against God in heaven. The little horn endeavors to usurp His authority with regard to the law and His prerogatives as the Creator; the little horn attempts to change the Sabbath. Antiochus Epiphanes did not go beyond the earthly limits of Jerusalem and his oppression did not affect the Sabbath. As for the allusion to the priest who is called *śār* in Daniel 8:9-12, we have understood that it applies to a heavenly being, Michael. This *śār* could hardly then be identified, as most critics think, with the priest Onias III who was murdered by Antiochus Epiphanes in 171.

3. Its nature: the little horn is described in Daniel's language as referring to a religious power which is not totally alien

to biblical tradition. Antiochus Epiphanes was only a political power and his religious claims were of a pagan character and had nothing to do with biblical tradition.

If the little horn, then, is not Antiochus Epiphanes, who else could it be? From 1844, looking back through the time, the vision reveals three periods of time and three dates which will help identify the little horn more specifically as the great culprit in religious history.

Three Periods of Time

The 1335 days are not the only period mentioned. It is not independent either; it is a part of a whole and relates to two other periods of time, 1260 days (a time, times, half a time), and 1290 days. The connection between these three prophecies is validated by several observations:

1. The 1335 days, the 1260 days, and the 1290 days cover more or less the same time span.
2. All of them are incorporated into the answer to the same question "How long until the end . . . ?" (Daniel 12:6) and therefore have the function of leading to the time of the end (Daniel 12:9).
3. All of them are related to preceding prophecies. The 1335 days refer to the 2300 evenings and mornings (see above). The 1290 days refer to the taking away of the daily sacrifices and to the desolation (Daniel 12:11; cf. 8:11, 13). The "time, two times, and half a time" of Daniel 12:7 refer, in Hebrew language, to the same prophecy conveyed in Aramaic by Daniel 7:25, "a time, times, and half a time."

Moreover, we find usage of the key word "understand" in Daniel 8 and 9.[86] Here, too, Daniel is left "without understanding" about the 1260 days (12:8; cf. 8:27). Then the same word reappears, "till the time of the end . . . the wise *shall understand*" (Daniel 12:9-10), in connection with two other measures of time, the 1290 days and 1335 days (Daniel 12:11-12). This phenomenon of "echo" between the "non-understanding" and the "understanding," the negative and the positive, as we have already pointed out, suggests a complementary relationship. The last two measures of time (1290 days and 1335 days) are answers to the perplexity that arises from the first measure (1260 days). The first lesson one can draw from this connection is that these periods have to be interpreted in terms of years. If the 1260 days are 1260 years, then it is the same for the 1290 days and 1335 days.

Furthermore, the way the 1290 days and the 1335 days are related indicates that these two periods are put in the same perspective, and the second period extends beyond the first one:

> And from the time that the daily sacrifice is taken away, and the abomination of desolation is set up, there shall be 1290 days; happy is he who waits, and comes to 1335 days.
>
> (Daniel 12:11-12)

So the 1290 days and the 1335 days start together, but the first period stops at 1290 days while the second period continues to 1335 days.

If we assume that 1844 is intended to be the final point of the 1335 days, then in order for us to find out the starting point of the 1335 days, we must subtract 1335 not from the number 1844—which includes the entire year 1844—but from the number of years which elapse *until* 1844, namely 1843 years[87] (1843-1335 = 508). According to our passage this date of 508 will mark the time when the daily sacrifice (or continual burning) is discontinued, in order "to set up the abomination of desolation" (Daniel 12:11).

Now, if the period of the 1290 days starts in 508, then it will end in 1798 (508 + 1290). We must notice, however, that although the two events, the taking away of the daily sacrifice, and the abomination of the desolation, are connected, they do not coincide. The first event prepares, and therefore precedes, the second, as the following literal translation suggests: "from the time of the taking away of the daily sacrifice so as to give (to set up) the abomination of the desolation" (Daniel 12:11; cf. 11:31).

In the book of Daniel, the expression "the abomination of the desolation" conveys the meaning of "oppressive power" (8:11, 13),[88] a power which the prophet sees exerted for 1260 days-years.

Since the oppressive power lasts 1260 years and works until 1798, the starting point of its action is then in 538 (1798-1260).

In summary:

- in 508 the little horn takes away the daily sacrifices;
- in 538 the little horn starts its oppression against the saints;
- in 1798 the little horn loses its power of oppression against the saints;
- in 1843-44 the time of waiting begins.

It is one thing to interpret the text by confining oneself to the task of exegesis; but at the end of the research it is another thing to come up with precise dates when dealing with a set of prophecies. We become apprehensive, then, because we are not only concerned with their reality in history, but also because interpretation of these dates implies the unpleasant and sad task of denunciation.

Indeed, the most dreadful accusation ever pronounced from the Bible is proclaimed by these dates. They speak of apostasy, of the usurpation of the rights and place of God, of oppression and intolerance. In addition, these dates are not "mystical,"[89] pointing to far-away ages, too far to be feared, or too external to our world to concern us. These dates are part of our world and our history. Hence our repulsion and natural skepticism.

Therefore, our examination of the history of these dates will be brief. It is neither healthy nor honorable to over-emphasize the outrages, crimes and mistakes, and to keep accusing *ad infinitum*. However, this should not prevent us from saying what must be said.

The prophet's word does not encumber itself with diplomatic maneuverings. Just as we should not condemn with a resentful or triumphant attitude, neither should we keep quiet.

Three Dates

By consulting history, it is revealed how relevant these dates are, how precisely they meet the prophetic perceptions of Daniel. We will now examine some of this history as it relates to the dates we have established.

In 508, with the help of a secular power, the ecclesiastical power of the little horn initiated its establishment on a political basis for the first time. It was the time when Clovis, King of France (481-511), the first heathen prince of that time to be converted (496? 506?), supplied the Church with the support of his government and his armies. It was the time when this "new Constantine," as he was nicknamed, had been victorious against the Visigoths; it was the first breakthrough into the Arian camp, the staunch enemy of the Church (507). These events "provided the papacy with a platform from which it was able to deploy its own government schemes safely."[90]

In 538, the same religious power freed itself from all who hampered its political establishment. In 508, the Arian camp was attacked for the first time, but we must wait until 538 (see Daniel 12:11) for the last Arian powers which had hitherto kept the Church from "political" establishment to be vanquished at last and expelled by the emperor Justinian (527-565).

Thus, as predicted by the prophecy (Daniel 7:24), the coming forth of this religious power entailed the fall of a number of kingdoms that had previously been part of the Roman Empire.

In fact, it was in 538 that Italy, the geographical seat of the Church, was liberated from the hands of the Ostrogoths, thereby allowing the Pontiffs to exert their power on every level.[91] The year 538, therefore, marks the period when papal supremacy is explicitly and universally acknowledged for the first time.[92] Consequently, it is the moment when the existing tendency to change the law becomes stronger and works with more assurance, authority and intolerance. The power of the Church is then free in its movements.

The year 1798 comes at the end of a series of events converging together,[93] including such events as the reformation movement, which shook off the yoke of the Church, the waves of the

Jesuits' rebellion, and the influence of philosophers such as Descartes and the encyclopedists Diderot and Voltaire, who propagated philosophical doubt and challenged the authority of the Church. And, finally, it included the French Revolution which rejected any ecclesiastical authority, founded a secular society, massacred Catholic priests and deified reason. Furthermore, in 1798 the Pope himself was arrested, stripped of every power and exiled. The foundation of the papal supremacy was then shaken.[94]

The Culprit

The charge has been suggested in the course of this argument. It may hurt and surprise many, yet it needs to be stated in order to be clear that this is indeed the Church, or rather, the Church in its political sense acting as a power of oppression and usurpation that we are discussing. We are not referring here to the thousands of sincere believers and priests at every level who were men and women of honor and great faith. They served the Church even though they disagreed with its acts. Neither are we referring here to the heroes and martyrs of the Church, who gave their lives and talents as a service of love, justice and truth. It is easy to lump everyone together and to charge all of them with the same crime; it is easy to fall into the base trap of prejudice and in the name of God point an accusing finger. It is the Church as an institution which the prophetic word denounces here, and not the people. It is only the Church, as a historical and political fact, which is the issue. Indeed, the power of the traditional Church in history discloses features which strangely remind us of the prophecy:

1. The character of the Church is both political and religious, as predicted in the symbolism of clay and the little horn with a human face (Daniel 2:42; 7:8, 24).

2. It comes forth on the political scene after the division of the Roman Empire into 10 kingdoms, three of which must yield their places to it (Daniel 2:42; 7:24; cf. Rev. 13).

3. It exercises oppressive power from 538 to 1798 (Daniel 7:25; 8:24; cf. Rev. 12:14; 13:5).

4. It attempts to change the heavenly law, especially the Sabbath (Daniel 7:25; 8:12; see also Rev. 14:9).

5. It purports to represent God and the City of God on earth, to judge, to forgive and save in the place of God (Daniel 7:25; 8:10, 11, 12, 25; see also Rev. 14:8).

We shall stop here and not extend this argument any further. Notice how discreetly the biblical text presents those painful times. However important and disturbing they may be (Daniel 7:25; 8:27), they are only an incident in the prophetic discourse, and in the end only serve one purpose—to provide hope. The prophecies of Daniel all have the same objective: to illuminate the end as a time of hope. In this respect, it is highly significant that since 1844 we have been able to go backward into time, and thereby check, so to speak, the correctness of the prophetic computation.

Yet a problem remains. In all honesty, we must raise it. Why 1844?

The prophetic calendar has met its historical application and the chronological milestones have been verified in regard to the events. In the year 31, Jesus of Nazareth died and no one today will question the historical and far-reaching importance of that event. The same holds true for 508, 538 and 1798; history attests that the prophetic word has been fulfilled. Something historical happened on those dates which allows us to check prophecy.

Yet, what happened in 1844 in our history which should assure us that we have not been dreaming, or carried away on the wings of some mystical or political speculation, or even by the impetus of dialectics? What will enable us, here on earth, to apprehend the truth of an event which prophecy locates precisely in heaven, i.e., beyond our control?

The Proclamation (Revelation 14)

John's Vision

At the Threshold of Revelation

Revelation, the last book of the biblical canon, will supply us with adequate light and will answer the puzzling question which arose from Daniel's vision of the last days. From the onset of the book we are already notified of this purpose. The first word, the title of the book, points directly to the end. "The Revelation of Jesus Christ" points to the Parousia.[95] Moreover, the blessing that introduces the reading of Revelation (1:3) and concludes the reading of Daniel (12:12) indicates the intention to couple the vision of John precisely with that of Daniel, in the same "waiting" for the end. The role played by the angel in the communication of the prophecy (Rev. 1:1) reminds us of the same process attested in chapters 8 and 9 of Daniel—showing again that the prophecy of Revelation stands in the same line as the visions of the Hebrew prophet.

The way the first vision of John takes up the thread of the last chapters of Daniel is also significant. Here again we find the same description of the Son of man (Rev. 1:13-15) as in Daniel[96] (Daniel 7:13; 10:4-6; 12:7), dressed in His priestly robe, devoid of any sacred ornaments. He is depicted in both passages as the High Priest officiating at Kippur (Lev. 16:3, 4).[97] Moreover, the mention of His hair "white like wool" (Rev. 1:14) is suggestive of the role this personage plays with regard to the judgment. In biblical and in ancient Jewish tradition this characteristic feature points to the God-Judge. Already the prophet Daniel mentioned it (7:9) and later the Talmud makes a particular symbol of it:

> God's hair is black (cf. Song 5:11) when He goes to war like a young man; his hair is white when He sits at the court, like an old man.
>
> (Hag. 14a)

The book of Revelation opens its cycle of visions at the judgment scene in association with the Day of Atonement.[98] Thus, the prophecy of Revelation starts in the perspective of the Parousia, with a direct reference to the prophecy of 2300 evenings and mornings of Daniel 8 in connection with the vision of the judgment of Daniel 7.

In the Heart of Revelation

The observation at the start of our reading of Revelation finds a vibrant confirmation in the very heart of this book. The chiastic structure in which the whole apocalyptic discourse is carried out[99] points to chapter 14 as being the entire book's center of gravity.[100] Chapter 14 is also the chapter on judgment. The word *krisis,* judgment (v. 7), is used here for the first time in the book, and the reference to the judgment occurs in the same sequence as in Daniel 7, i.e., after the beasts and before the coming of the Son of man. Thus, chapter 14 plays the same role in the book of Revelation as chapter 7 in the book of Daniel; the parallelism is striking.

Furthermore, the same alternate movement of the prophet's gaze between heaven and earth, which Daniel developed in a similar context of concern, is also expressed here in the literary unit of Rev. 14 and 15.

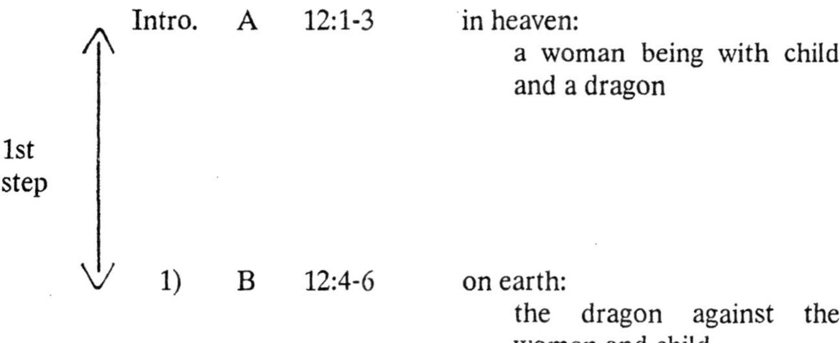

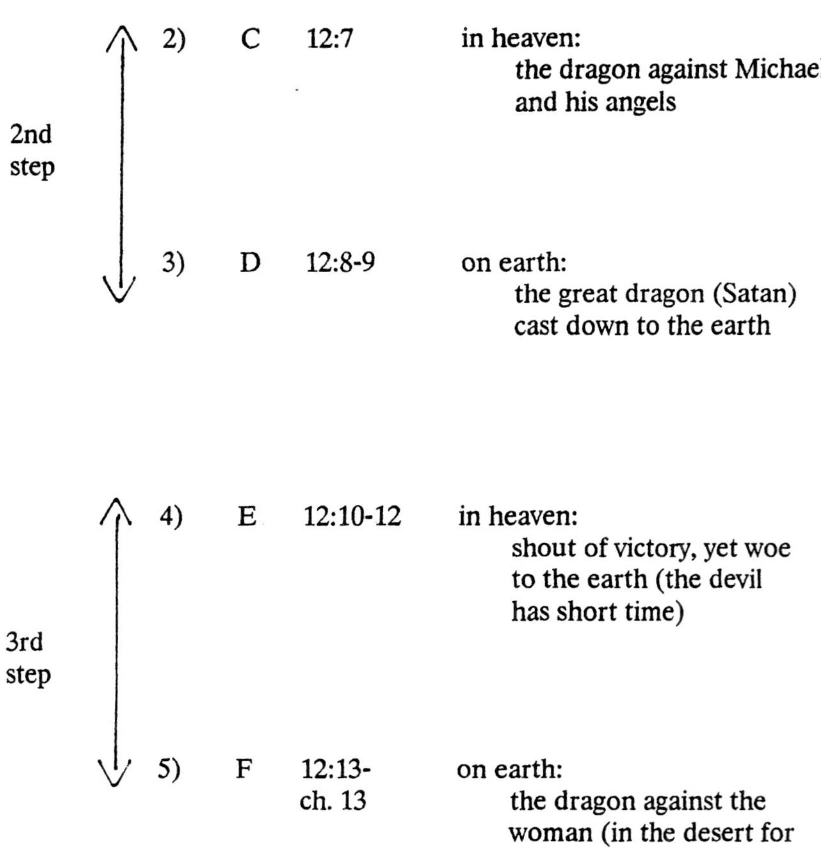

Step	No.		Reference	Description
2nd step	2)	C	12:7	in heaven: the dragon against Michael and his angels
	3)	D	12:8-9	on earth: the great dragon (Satan) cast down to the earth
3rd step	4)	E	12:10-12	in heaven: shout of victory, yet woe to the earth (the devil has short time)
	5)	F	12:13-ch. 13	on earth: the dragon against the woman (in the desert for time, times and half a time, vv. 13-17); the beast empowered by the dragon (13:2) to fight God and the saints (persecution for 42 months, vv. 5, 7); another beast endowed with authority by the preceding beast and the dragon (13:11-12) against God and the saints (13:15)

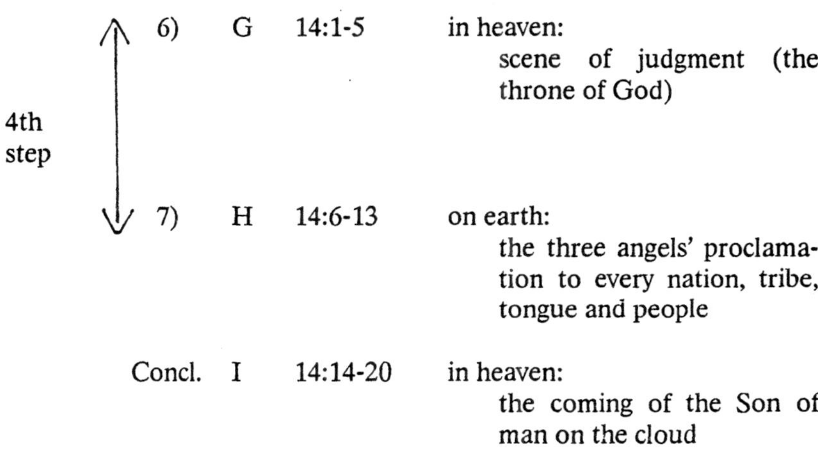

4th step	6)	G	14:1-5	in heaven: scene of judgment (the throne of God)
	7)	H	14:6-13	on earth: the three angels' proclamation to every nation, tribe, tongue and people
	Concl.	I	14:14-20	in heaven: the coming of the Son of man on the cloud

The evolution of the conflict, developed in 4 steps,[101] reveals once again that earth's history is accompanied by a parallel movement in heaven:

In the first step, B on earth relates to A in heaven on the common motif of the woman and child.

In the second step, D on earth relates to C in heaven on the common motif of the dragon being overcome by Michael.

In the third step, F on earth relates to E in heaven on the common motif of the dragon threatening the earth.

In the fourth step, H on earth relates to G in heaven on the common motif of judgment.

Note that I, which features the coming of the Son of man "in heaven," has no counterpart on earth; the reason is simply because henceforth history is no longer human, but belongs to another order.

The fourth step deserves particular attention within our specific concern. The proclamation of Judgment and Creation on earth (H) is paired with the heavenly vision which must be interpreted as the judgment scene (G).[102]

Moreover, the reference to the judgment comes precisely along the same line as in Daniel 7. Here as there it is preceded by the coming of a beast with ten horns[103] which has the qualities of the four beasts of Daniel 7[104] (the lion, the bear, the leopard and the beast with 10 horns). It is also characterized by the same power of oppression and usurpation of God's rights (cf. Daniel 7:25); and here as there it immediately precedes the coming of the Son of man on the cloud[105] (Daniel 7:13-14).

The vision of Daniel 7 and the three angels' messages of Revelation 14 are then situated at the same level in the prophetic line. The judgment in heaven predicted in Daniel 7 and the shout of the three messengers of Revelation 14 coincide.

Judgment and Creation

In the very first words of the first message one can detect a strong reference to the judgment:

> Fear God and give glory to Him, for the hour of His *judgment* has come.
>
> (Rev. 14:7a)

But there is more—here the judgment is associated with Creation:

> And worship Him who *made heaven and earth,* the sea and springs of water.
>
> (Rev. 14:7b)

This association of Judgment with Creation is particularly significant. It is a clear reference to the Day of Atonement, the unique day when the Israelite traditionally associates Judgment with Creation.

The Evidence of the Bible

The entire Bible attests the very function of the Day of Atonement as pointing to Creation and Judgment. It is the Pentateuch that conveys this testimony most eloquently; indeed, it seems that the whole text is dedicated to this theme. In the Pentateuch, Creation and Judgment are the two landmarks around which the book revolves. The word moves back and forth, from Creation to Judgment, from Judgment to Creation, and so on:

Creation:	Gen. 1-2 (the two Creation stories)
Judgment:	Gen. 6-7 (the flood)
Creation:	Gen. 8-9 (recreation after the flood)[106]
Judgment:	Gen. 11 (the tower of Babel)
Creation:	Gen. 12:1-3 (the call of Abraham)[107]
Judgment:	Ex. 6-11 (the ten plagues)
Creation:	Ex. 12-Lev. (the Exodus and the tabernacle)[108]
Judgment:	Num. 14 (the sentence: they shall not see the land)
Creation:	Deut. 34 (perspective of the promised land, allusion to Moses' resurrection)[109]

Thus the Creation-to-Judgment pattern creates the framework of the Pentateuch, thereby indicating the keynote of its five books. Is it then accidental that the center of the Pentateuch—Leviticus 16—deals precisely with the Day of Atonement, which presupposes Creation and Judgment? Not only is the book of Leviticus the center of the Pentateuch,[110] but Leviticus 16 is also the exact center of the book itself.[111] This literary phenomenon testifies to the connection existing between the Day of Atonement and its components—Creation and Judgment.

The same lesson is conveyed by the Prophets, especially in the book of Jonah. This book belongs to the liturgy of the Day of Atonement[112] and is indeed concerned with God's atonement and forgiveness (Jonah 4:2, 11). It also bases its message upon a reference to Creation (1:9; 2:3) and Judgment (1:2; 3:4-10).

In the book of Daniel the peculiar expression "evenings and mornings" (Daniel 8:14) which is attached to the Day of Atonement, may also refer to the Creation story, the only passage other than the one referred to in this study using this very expression (Gen.

1:5, 8, 13, 19, 23, 31). Thus, the association of Creation with Judgment in Daniel 8:14, points to Judgment by the parallelism with Daniel 7 and to Creation by means of the words "evenings and mornings."[113]

This theme is also markedly conveyed in the Psalms. For example, Psalm 103, which is concerned with the Day of Atonement,[114] brings up Creation (vv. 4, 5, 14, 22) and Judgment (vv. 17-19). God is described there as Creator and Father (v. 13), but also as a king judging on his throne (v. 19). Outside of Psalm 103, the rest of the book of Psalms witnesses to this same concept. There, God is worshiped as the Creator who "fashions the hearts" (Ps. 33:15a) and therefore the God who is able to evaluate and judge "the works of man" (Ps. 33:15b; cf. Ps. 7:9-11). God is worshiped as the Judge whose throne has "righteousness and justice for foundation" (Ps. 89:14), but also as the Creator of the heavens and the earth (Ps. 89:9-12). Enshrined in the heart of the Bible, the Psalms—which were sung on the *doukhan*,[115] the sacred platform of the temple—were to reflect the feelings of the people prostrated before their Judge.

The Evidence of the Jewish Tradition

In the wake of the Bible, Jewish tradition has faithfully interpreted the Day of Atonement as a double reference to Creation and Judgment.

> There was an evening, there was a morning, unique day, this means that the Blessed be He, gave them (to Israel), a unique day which was nothing but the Day of Atonement.
>
> (*Midrash Rabbah*, Gen. IV, 10)

The reference to Gen 1:5 in connection to the Day of Atonement suggests that actually the birth of Kippur coincides with that of the universe. Creation and the Day of Atonement belong to the same world of thought in Jewish tradition. Moreover, the tradition links the Day of Atonement to the Day of Judgment, the moment when God's forgiveness seals the destiny of the repented.

> To average people, who are neither perfectly righteous, nor totally wicked, will be granted a delay of 10 days (from the first to the tenth of Tishri); they have then until Kippur to repent, in which case they will live; otherwise death will sanction their bad behavior.
>
> (T. B., *Rosh Hashana* 16b)

Parallel to these traditions, the prayers which are said during the Day of Atonement testify, this time on a liturgical level, to this double reference to Creation and Judgment. The first prayers carry the believer into the spirit of the festival, professing faith in Creation and hoping for forgiveness in Judgment.

> Blessed be thou, Lord our God, King of the universe, who opens the doors to mercy and gives light to the eyes of those who expect forgiveness from the One who creates light and darkness, and creates everything.
>
> (Yotser leyom Kippur)

Throughout the liturgy the awareness of the God-Judge who discloses everything is paired with the truth that He is the Creator:

> How could man be just before his Creator, as everything is disclosed to Him?
>
> (Mosaph leyom Kippour)

Moreover, as an echo to the message of Revelation 14, an interesting detail is to be noted. The prayers recited on the Day of Atonement urge one to fear God, by precisely referring to Creation and Judgment (emphasis supplied).

> Spread the *fear* of thy name, Lord our God, over all thy *creatures,* that all men may *fear* thee and that all those thou hast created may prostrate before thee. . . . For we know, Lord our God, that Sovereignty is thine,

> power is in thy hand and thy dreadful name impresses all those thou hast created.
>
> (*Shulkhan Aruch*, ch. CIC, 582)

> We must give this day all its holiness because it is a day of fear and awe. In this day thy reign is established and thy throne is made firm . . . . For thou art the *judge*, the pleader, and the witness, the one who opens and seals. And thou shalt remember every forgiven thing and thou shalt open the book of remembrance. . . , then the great shofar will be sounded, and the small still voice will be heard, the angels will shudder from *fear* and say "This is the Day of Judgment."
>
> (*Book of prayers*, Mahzor min rosh Hashana weyom hakippurim, I. p. 31)

We also find the association of Creation-Judgment in the traditional connection between the Day of Atonement (10 Tishri) and the New Year's Day (*Rosh Hashana*, the first of Tishri). As *The Jewish Encyclopedia* puts it:

> On the first of Tishri, the sacred New Year's Day and the anniversary of creation, man's doings were judged and his destiny was decided; and on the tenth of Tishri the decree of heaven was sealed.
>
> (Vol. 2, p. 281; cf. Tosef. 13; R. H. 11a, 16a)

Actually the two festivals seem to have been associated from the most ancient times and even belong to a single celebration. It is the same ritual which characterizes them, the same sacrifices (Num. 29:1-5, 8-11), the same sounds of the shofar (Lev. 25:9; 23:24).[116]

All this information collected from the Bible and Jewish tradition seemingly points out a specific background against which the message of Revelation 14 is outlined. The association of Creation and Judgment indeed refers to the Day of Atonement.

The Usurpation of Judgment

The second message is a mourning lament (cf. Jer. 51:8):

> Babylon is fallen, is fallen, that great city, because she has made all nations drink of the wine of the wrath of her fornication.
>
> (Rev. 14:8)

The prophetic word is no longer an appeal; it is a sad observation. The messenger does not address men anymore in order to bring them to God's side; his face is now turned against Babel, the staunch enemy of God, to denounce it and predict its end.

The name of Babylon (in Hebrew, Babel) is in itself significant; it reminds us of the foolish enterprise of those men who designed a tower whose top was to reach the "gate of God." That was the first meaning of the word *bab-el*. The builders' intention was clear. In biblical language, "to possess the gate" of someone means to control or dominate him, and ultimately to take over his place (Gen. 22:17; 24:60).[117] All the powers of earth came and were united together in order to achieve this absurd enterprise, to take over God's place. Henceforth Babylon (Babel) would become the symbol of this proud but doomed attempt to usurp the place of the heavenly God (see Is. 14:4-23; 48:20; Jer. 51:9-11; cf. Rev. 17:5; 18:10; etc.).

Thus the accusation of Revelation is implicit in the name Babel, and recurs with an emphasis on the charge: "She has made all nations drink of the wine of the wrath of her fornication" (Rev. 14:8). In the following verses the expression "the wine of the wrath" explicitly applies to the *Judgment* of God (vv. 8-10). To say that Babel made nations drink "of the wine of her wrath" means that she tried to take God's place precisely in regard to the Judgment (cf. Jer. 25:15ff.).

Again, this is the same type of accusation which Daniel's vision brings against the little horn which "exalted himself as high as the Prince of the host" (8:11). It is also noteworthy that the root of the word "exalted" (*gdl*) is the same as the one used in Gen. 11:4 to designate the "tower" (*migdāl*) of Babel. The description of the little horn's behavior reminds us, through the etymological play on words, of the "escalation" of Babel.

Moreover, the power with the same characteristics as the little horn in Daniel 11 (see v. 36) happens to come from the North (see v. 29), which is another way of referring to Babylon by the prophets (cf. Jer. 1:14; 46:13, 20; 50:1, 3; Ez. 26:7; etc.).[118]

The two figures are identical even in their motivation. In Daniel 8, the ambition of the little horn is to exalt himself to the position of the Prince of the heavenly host, who is the High Priest officiating on the Day of Atonement. In Revelation 14, the ambition of Babel is to take the place of the God-Judge. Since the Judgment and the Day of Atonement are the same event, it follows that the places coveted by the little horn and Babel are the same. Note in this connection the phrase "Who is like the beast" (Rev. 13:4) which is an echo of "Who is like God" (*Mikael*). It thereby indicates the nature of the usurpation of the beast, namely, the pretense of taking the place of the High Priest Michael.

The ambition of Babel is identical to that of the little horn. It is of a religious nature and is aimed at the position of the High Priest in connection with Kippur and the Judgment. Thus it is *the power to forgive sins and ultimately to decide about salvation* (see Lev. 16:39, 32) that both are striving for.

Through the prophecy of the 2300 evenings and mornings the pretension of Babel and the lies of the little horn are finally disclosed. This is indicated through the connection made in Daniel 8 between the cleansing of the sanctuary and the "vision concerning the continual." This connection comes out in the question/answer between the two angels.

Question:

> How long will the vision be, concerning the continual and the transgression of desolation, the giving of both the sanctuary and the host to be trampled under foot?
>
> (Daniel 8:13)

Answer:

> For two thousand three hundred days; then the sanctuary shall be cleansed.
>
> (Daniel 8:14)

What Daniel calls "the vision concerning the continual"[119] refers to an event which has already been described in Daniel 8:11, where it is said that the little horn will take away the continual sacrifice. In Daniel 8:13-14 this event is denounced in terms of "transgression" and "desolation." The text not only shows the negative connotation this action conveys, but it also proclaims it as a crime.

The role of the continual sacrifice is, as we have already indicated, to represent God on earth (Ex. 29:42-44). The taking away of this continual sacrifice by the little horn betrays his intention to represent God on earth; this is his crime.

If, in order to answer the question "How long will the vision be, concerning the continual?" the angel refers to a heavenly Kippur, this does not specify *when* the continual sacrifice will end. The answer to the question of the continual sacrifice does not stand on a *time* level, but on the level of its *nature*. By staying on that level, the angel's answer suggests that the continual sacrifice belongs to the same heavenly order as the cleansing of the sanctuary. The angel's intention is once again to denounce the lies of the little horn. The reference to a heavenly Day of Atonement implies the difficult concept of a heavenly ritual. Connecting the Day of Atonement and the continual sacrifice and putting them on the same level amounts to saying that the continual sacrifice normally belongs to the same heavenly order. The lie and imposture of the little horn is then declared and identified.

Thus the Vision of the End fulfills a double function; not only does it indicate the time and place of the Day of Atonement and Judgment, but it denounces the nature of the pretension of the little horn, the power of Babel. This is what the second message of Revelation 14 is for, to denounce the pretension and the lie of Babel. Babel is now judged.

Of course, Babel still remains alive on earth, and its activities go on beyond 1844. But this is the time when the lie is unveiled and therefore when the fate of Babel is suggested. "She is fallen" (Rev. 14:8). This word is characteristic of the language of prophets: it is by means of a *perfectum propheticum* that the inexorable fall is foretold.[120] The event is so certain that it is seen as if it had already happened.

The prophecy of Revelation 14 concerning Babel does not refer so much to her fall as to the sentence pronounced at the time of judgment. Here the second message parallels the vision of the prophet Daniel (7:11, 12). He also discovered "in the books" that on the Day of Judgment the little horn would receive the same fatal sentence and reported it in the same language.

The Usurpation of Creation

The third message is heard as a threat, in the same "loud voice" as the first message.

> If anyone worships the beast and his image, and receives his mark on his forehead or on his hand, he himself shall also drink of the wine of the wrath of God, which is poured out full strength into the cup of his indignation. . . . Here is the patience of the saints; here are those who keep the commandments of God and the faith of Jesus.
>
> (Rev. 14:9-12)

The beast which is worshiped is the same as the one depicted in Revelation 13. These passages share many common themes (cf. 13:4, 8, 15, 16, 17). Here too, the beast is worshiped; here too, we are told about his image and his mark on the forehead or on the hand.

Moreover, the behavior of the beast of Revelation 13 reminds us of the little horn in Daniel 7 and 8 (7:8, 11, 25; cf. 8:25, etc.).

> And he was given a mouth speaking great things and blasphemies.
>
> (Rev. 13:5; read vv. 4-8)

The beast of Revelation 14, the beast of Revelation 13 and the little horn of Daniel 7 and 8 represent the same figure, which we already denounced as having the mentality of Babel. Here it also shows the same intentions toward the divine.

Whereas in the first message, it is God as the Creator who is *worshiped,* "worship Him who made heaven and earth . . ." (v. 7), in the third message it is the beast that is *worshiped,* "those who worship the beast . . ." (vv. 9, 11). The third message thereby indicates the nature of the usurpation; the beast takes to itself the prerogatives of the God-Creator, and it is worshiped.

Curiously, this worship of the beast shows up through "a mark on the forehead or on the hand" (vv. 9, 11). This image is particularly vivid and suggestive for the Israelite because it points to the signs of his faithfulness to the commandments of God.

> And these words which I command you today shall be in your heart. . . . You shall bind them as a sign on your hand, and they shall be as frontlets between your eyes.
>
> (Deut. 6:6-8; cf. 11:18; cf. Ex. 13:9)

This requirement, which pervaded the daily religious life of the Israelite, was certainly uppermost in the mind of John. The same thought is also implied at the end of the speech where the saints are characterized as "those who keep the commandments of God" (Rev. 14:12).

We should not be surprised to find out that this text reflects a concern for the law of God. The reference to the law of God is implied by the Day of Atonement, which stands in the background of our passage. It is significant that atonement was made by the process of sprinkling the blood on the ark containing the Ten Commandments.[121] The atonement consisted of more than the mere erasing of the fault; along with the mercy and forgiveness represented in the sprinkled blood, it implied the "control" of justice as expressed in the engraved law of God. Forgiveness implies the consciousness of sin, hence the reference to justice. The requirement of *ṣedeq* (justice) is also inherent in Kippur. One wonders whether the exceptional usage of the word *niṣdaq* (to be declared just) as used in Daniel 8:14 to designate the process of Kippur (cleansing of the Sanctuary), was meant to emphasize the imperative reference to the law, the expression of *ṣedeq* (see Ps. 119:172). It is on this law that the power of Babel will focus its energies.

By association,[122] our passage suggests a focus on the usurpation of the beast. The beast wants to take God's place as the Creator, and wants to replace His commandments by his own. Since the usurpation of God's place is linked with faith in Creation and with keeping the commandments of God our passage seems to point by association to the Sabbath. If this interpretation of Rev. 14:9-11 is right, then we are correct in thinking that the accusation of Dan. 7:25 against the little horn, to "change times and law," may point as well to the Sabbath. Not only does the association of time-law give room for the perception of this allusion to the Sabbath,[123] but it is also noteworthy that the very concept of "changing time" has been traditionally associated with the Sabbath in Jewish liturgy.[124] Worship of the beast and faithfulness to its laws (see Rev. 13:15-17) are made a substitute for the worship of God and faithfulness to His commandments. The transfer is all the easier as the new requirement uses the old one as a prototype. This is the same imagery of a "mark" on the forehead and hand. The similarity in language not only indicates a substitution with regard to the commandments of God, but also suggests that the new law is molded on the old one.

On the level of history, we have been able to check the accuracy of the apocalyptic vision. Sunday has been substituted for the Sabbath, the commandment given by God to commemorate the Creation event.[125] The commandment which stipulated the observance of the seventh day seemed to be preserved. The mold was the same; only the dough was new. The seventh day shifted to the first.

The observance of one day rather than another may seem quite peculiar and even ridiculous in comparison with the importance of the issue at stake. Yet, what may appear as trivial denotes, in fact, a profound difference. Respect for the Sabbath as the day which has been determined by the Creator, and not for the other day which has been decreed by human tradition, indicates the loyalty of the believer. It is from above only, from the Absolute, that the believer draws his value system. By keeping the Sabbath, the sign of belonging to God (Ex. 31:12-17; Ezek. 20:12[126]), the believer, remarkably, becomes a sign himself—a sign that the kingdom to which he belongs is not of the world, but of God.

The break of the Sabbath has nothing to do with a weekly vacation; it is the concrete expression of faith in Creation, the sign of one's dependence on heaven. When that is well understood, the keeping of the Sabbath excludes any trend to legalism or formalism. As the absolute sign of faith in the God of heaven, the Sabbath carries in itself the view that salvation is only from above.

On the opposite end stands the mentality of Babel, made up of culture, tradition and the "works" of men. Sometimes the process is so insidious that it may even occur within the keeping of the Sabbath, within the pretension of a reference to the law of God, but with the eager concern to build one's salvation with one's own bricks.

* * * *

The three angels message evolves around the reference to Judgment and Creation. The first angel utters his message in a positive manner; it is an exhortation. The other two convey the same truth by opposition to the power who wants to usurp God's prerogatives; it is an open accusation, the second message by reference to Judgment and the third message by reference to Creation. It is noteworthy that the same sequence Judgment-Creation which is indicated in the first message reappears in the second (Judgment) and the third message (Creation). This not only confirms the idea that the second and the third messages take over the same two themes of the first message, but also reminds us of the Spirit of the Day of Atonement.

It is remarkable that the sequence is Judgment-Creation and not the reverse, as would have been expected according to the chronological order. On the Day of Atonement the awareness of

Judgment precedes that of Creation; standing before his Judge the believer realizes that he stands before his Creator. For only the Creator knows the intricacies of the heart.

Indeed, the message of Judgment and Creation may be understood as a reference to the Day of Atonement and its proclamation may be perceived as the earthly counterpart of the heavenly Day of Atonement. Three observations lead us to this conclusion:

1) The sequence of motifs in Rev. 13-14 parallels the sequence of motifs in Dan. 7 putting the earthly proclamation of this message at the same place as the heavenly Day of Judgment (= Day of Atonement).

2) The literary structure of Rev. 12-14 develops a movement in four steps, each step having a heavenly side and an earthly one; the fourth step puts together the earthly proclamation of Judgment and Creation and the heavenly scene of the throne of God and the Judgment.

3) The content of the message Judgment-Creation points to the theological content of the Day of Atonement.

Since this proclamation is supposed to take place on earth at the time of the end—more precisely, since 1844—we may well consider this historical event as an indication—seen from earth—of the heavenly event, the Judgment, the Day of Atonement. This observation confirms the vision of the prophet Daniel. Parallel to the heavenly Day of Atonement, Daniel had seen an earthly time of waiting and hope (Daniel 12:12).

CHAPTER THREE

A VISION OF WAR

"At the time of the end the King of the South shall attack him, and the King of the North shall come against him."
Daniel 11:40

The whole book of Daniel is pervaded with tension which inexorably involves two camps in a merciless war. From chapter 1, we immediately enter into the conflict. Babylon is opposed to Jerusalem (Daniel 1:1), and the words which are used there point beyond the mere local conflict which brought Israel into exile. Through the rare word "*Šin'ār*" (Daniel 1:2, which is the antique name of Babel,[127] as preserved in Gen. 11:2), the author alludes to another conflict of a spiritual order.

Indeed, the story continues with the setting up of the two camps. On one side is Babel, attempting to usurp the authority of the God of Israel. The King of Babel intends to make Daniel and his companions worship him according to the Babylonian religion, and wants to change their names accordingly. On the other side stand Daniel and his companions, who resist Babylonian alienation and adhere to their God. Against the king who "appointed" food from pagan worship,[128] Daniel "purposed" in his heart not to defile himself. The same Hebrew verb *wayyaśem* is used for "purposed" (1:8) and the "giving" of their new names (1:7). Thus the text suggests that their decision not to eat had to do with their faithfulness to God and their identity.[129] Moreover, the verb "appointed" (in its form *wayᵉman*, 1:5) has only God the Creator as its subject (Jonah 2:1; 4:6, 7, 8). Therefore Daniel responded to the King's order by asking for the food appointed by the Creator (Daniel 1:12). Actually, the association of the three words "vegetables given to eat" which is brought out in Daniel 1:12 recurs only in Gen. 1:29, thereby suggesting a hint at the text of the Creation story. This first incident in Daniel's exilic experience will set the scene for the whole book.

In chapters 3 and 6, the two camps confront each other again in the same conflict. The story is always the same claim for God's place by Babel, which demands worship (3:6, 10, 11, 14; 6:7, 13), and always the same resistance from the camp of Daniel (3:12, 16-18; 6:10, 20). The outcome is again the same; God sends His angel (3:28; 6:22), and God's victory terminates the conflict (3:25-29; 6:22-28).

Inserted between chapters 3 and 6, the events reported in chapters 4 and 5 display the situation in a different manner. Only the pagan monarchs are on the stage, yet the two opposite powers are still involved in the same conflict. Both Nebuchadnezzar and Belshazzar "lift themselves up against the Lord of heaven" (5:23; 4:30; cf. 37), and the beastly state and the metallic chains which draw toward the earth are opposed to the spiritual, which lifts up and gives humanity[130] (4:15, 23, 32-33 versus vv. 34, 36; 5:2, 4, 23b versus vv. 5, 24). In a parallel way the kingdoms of metals (chapter 2) and of beasts (chapters 7, 8) are opposed to the heavenly kingdom (2:34, 44; 7:13, 14; 8:11, 25).

The more we progress into the book of Daniel, the more explicit and larger the conflict becomes. In chapters 7 and 8 the first ingredients of a universal war are laid down. Hitherto the conflict was rather local and essentially concerned either Israel or Daniel. The conflict now overflows beyond the frontiers of space, time, and nations, to involve heavenly powers. Now the two camps are well defined, the saints and God on one side, and the little horn and the nations claiming the place of God on the other side.

In chapter 9, the conflict takes on a cosmic dimension revolving around two supernatural princes. The passage dealing with the 70-weeks prophecy sets the Messiah Prince of v. 25a over against the aggressing prince of v. 26b. And the second prince comes against the first one not only as his adversary but also as his usurper; he wants to take his place. Significantly he bears the same name (*nāgîḏ*), a term which is also applied in Ez. 28:2 to a demonic and cosmic power.[131] This passage is not only similar in common wording and patterns of thoughts with Daniel 9:24-27, but it is also the only other biblical reference carrying this association of *nāgîḏ-mšḥ* (Ezek. 28:14).[132]

In chapter 10, the figure of a heavenly prince appears again, named for the first time—this is Michael—and for the first time involved in the war (10:13, 21). The end of the times is now in the offing (10:14), and the last step of human history is described as a gigantic war, *ṣābāʾ gādôl* (Daniel 10:1). In this connection, the parallel between Daniel praying and fasting on earth during three weeks (10:4) and the heavenly battle involving supernatural powers during the same period of time (10:13) suggests the nature of the impending war.[133] The battle will take place on both fronts, heaven and earth, implying again a special connection between the two. Indeed the ground has been carefully prepared. Everything is directed toward this unavoidable conclusion.

Tied with chapter 10,[134] chapter 11 contains the climax of the tension pervading the entire book. This last step is decisive; it is therefore expected that the battle will rage more fiercely than ever. Finally the prophet's vision goes beyond the mere information *about* a conflict; it reveals the nature of the war and the issue at stake.

The Nature of the War

Situation in Time

Daniel 11:1-4 functions as an introduction to the chapter and situates the time of the conflict dealt with in the rest of chapter 11 (vv. 5-45). From the very beginning, the prophecy provides clues, by using the kings in history as landmarks.

v. 2: Three more kings shall arise in Persia; and a fourth shall be far richer than all of them; and when he has become strong through his riches, he shall stir up all against the kingdom of Greece.

v. 3: Then a mighty king shall arise, who shall rule with great dominion and do according to his will.

v. 4: And when he has arisen, his kingdom shall be broken and divided toward the four winds of heaven, but not to his posterity, nor according to the dominion with which he ruled; for his kingdom shall be plucked up and go to others besides these. (Daniel 11:2-4, RSV)

The first questions which surface on reading these mysterious words are, who are the first three kings, and particularly, who is the fourth one?

Considering the fact that these four kings are from the kingdom of Persia and that we are still in the days of Cyrus (suzerain of Darius the Mede; see Daniel 10:1), it can be deduced from history[135] that the first three kings after Cyrus are successively Cambyses, Darius,[136] Ahasuerus, and that the fourth is none other than Artaxerxes; a view which has been adopted in Jewish tradition.[137]

Indeed, history confirms this choice; Artaxerxes has been referred to as the one "who more cleverly [than his predecessors] did his best to win among them [the great cities] allies for money, and to weaken them by inciting them to make war with each other."[138] Likewise another historian describes Artaxerxes' involvement in these terms:

> The Greeks, Persia realized, might be annoying, but they could never seriously hurt Persia, as long as they remained divided among themselves and fought each other incessantly. Persia learned therefore to keep those fights going and *she spent money* freely with that end in view.
>
> By the time Artaxerxes I died in 424 B.C., Persia had the satisfaction of seeing the Greek cities lining up in a kind of miniature World War. The whole Greek world flung itself behind the two chief cities, Athens and Sparta, who proceeded to fight each other to the death.[139] (Emphasis supplied)

Artaxerxes is thus the one who fits the description made by the prophecy of Daniel, "Through his riches, he shall stir up all against the realm of Greece" (11:2). Notice that he is not especially perceived as fighting the Greeks but rather as weakening them by the means of great sums of money.[140]

Why four kings? and why has the prophecy started with the fourth one and not with another? Artaxerxes has already been pointed out in the book of Daniel in connection with the prophecy of the seventy weeks (Daniel 9:24-27); it started with the decree of Artaxerxes. Moreover, the very first words of Daniel 11:1 remind of the introduction of Daniel 9.[141] This same setting of Daniel 9 at the opening of chapter 11 indicates that the prophet clearly connects his vision to the 70 weeks, hence also in the wake of the 2300 days, since both periods start at the decree of Artaxerxes.

This reference to the decree of Artaxerxes on the eve of the conflict which follows, has a particular meaning. Just as God controls history[142] in order to guide it towards the cross in Daniel 9, and towards the time of the end in Daniel 8, He will also control history through the great conflict.

What follows (vv. 3, 4) is more easily understood. There is unanimous agreement in the identification of Alexander the great as the mighty king.[143] It is indeed the same power as that perceived in Daniel 8:8. The whole phrase used in vv. 4 and 40 in Hebrew is patterned on that of Daniel 8:8.[144]

Moreover, Daniel 11:4 describes the same history as Daniel 8:8. After a period of domination (cf. Daniel 7:6; 2:39), the kingdom is divided into four kingdoms. Thus Daniel 11:3, 4 takes over the prophecy mentioned in Daniel 8:8 concerning the same power, that is, the Greek empire in its splendor (Alexander) and in its decline (the four divisions).

As the prophecy of Daniel 11 continues, it informs us that the power passes to other hands; "his kingdom shall be broken and divided toward . . . posterity, nor according to the dominion with which he ruled; for his kingdom shall be plucked up and go to others besides these" (Daniel 11:4b).

What does "these" mean? The plural form of the demonstrative pronoun (*'ēlleh*) indicates that "these" points back to the four kingdoms just mentioned above. By saying that the dominion will be given "to others than these" the text implies that the dominion will be given to a power coming *after* the four divisions which stand for the hellenistic period. This new power is therefore to be identified as Rome. Some interpreters think that *'ēlleh* (these) refers to Alexander's generals, implying the rise of other kingdoms besides those ruled by these four generals. They are identified as the dynasties of Armenia and Cappadocia, which took their independence 150 years after Alexander's death.[145] The biblical text does not support such an interpretation. The only plural word which the *'ēlleh* can refer to is "four winds of heaven" in the same language as in Daniel 8:8 (cf. 7:6). Actually the division affects the whole empire of Alexander for the specific expression "towards the four winds of heaven" implies totality. The reference to the independent kingdoms of Armenia and Cappadocia is then excluded since those inherit only a part of Alexander's kingdom. "Others than these," then, can only refer to something coming *after* the four kingdoms, since "these" receive the whole succession. In addition to that, the Hebrew word translated here by "posterity" (*'aḥᵃrîṯ*) is always used in the book of Daniel in a temporal sense (Dan 8:1, 9, 23; 10:14; 12:8).[146] Rather than implying the mere posterity, i.e. generated children, *'aḥᵃrîṯ* points to something coming after, chronologically speaking. The idea is that the dominion will be handed over to a power coming next after the kingdom of Greece. Since what comes after the kingdom of Greece is the hellenistic period, the dominion is given to what comes after it, which is Rome.

Moreover, the kingdom which succeeds the four is described as being disconnected from the preceding kingdoms. This new kingdom is characterized by its essential difference. It is "*others* than these." We are familiar with such language; it reminds us of the fourth kingdom of Daniel 7 which is described as "different" and is identified as the Roman Empire (see Daniel 7:7b, 23). Why, then, do we pass so quickly over Rome, which is barely suggested here? Having in mind the connection between chapter 8 and chapter 11, we should not be surprised that here, as there, the reference to Rome has been expedited by the author, anxious in both passages to come to the next stage. Thus "given to others besides these" (Daniel 11:4b) means "given to Rome."

The period which follows Daniel 11:5 indicates a new step in both form and substance (see below), and therefore should come chronologically after the Roman Empire.[147] This is the reason why the writer cannot follow the generally accepted interpretation[148] which assigns the powers of the North and South to the Seleucids and Ptolemies kingdoms. The period covered by the conflict which Daniel 11:5-39 narrates is thus the same as that covered by the little horn in Daniel 7 and 8 and by the toes of the feet in Daniel 2. The correlation works particularly in regard to chapter 8 where the section about the little horn comes at the same place in the sequence (see the parallelism of structure between ch. 8 and 11 as pointed out in our Introduction). It is also noteworthy that the power of the North, as it is described in Dan. 11:5-45, features a number of striking similarities with the little horn of Daniel 7 and 8 and also with the peoples of Daniel 2 as referred to by the feet of the image. Here again we find the same aggressive action against God and His saints (Daniel 11:28, 35, 41; cf. 7:21, 25; 8:9-12, 24, 25), and against the sanctuary (Daniel 11:31; cf. 8:11, 13). Here again we find the same characteristic features and the same ambitions: pride and presumption (Daniel 11:12, 36; cf. 7:8, 20, 25; 8:25), prosperity (Daniel 11:23, 36; cf. 7:21; 8:12, 24), and usurping of God's power (Daniel 11:36, 37; cf. 7:25; 8:11).

The end of the power of the North is also described in Daniel 11 in terms that remind one of the little horn (cf. Daniel 8:25) and the statue of Daniel 2 (Daniel 2:45).

Daniel 2:45	(The earthly kingdoms are broken) not by human hand.
Daniel 8:25b	(The little horn shall be broken) not by human hand.
Daniel 11:45	(The power of the North shall come to its end) with no one to help him.

The coincidental relationship of the power of the North with the little horn and the feet of clay is not limited to the field of similarities only, but it also appears in the way this power begins and ends. It so happens that its advent takes place at *exactly the same moment as the others*, precisely after the Roman Empire. Furthermore, this interpretation is confirmed by the chiastic structure which relates chapter 11 and 12 of Daniel,[149] more specifically connecting Daniel 11:5-39 to Daniel 12:5-11 (see below B and B_1).

A	Dan. 11:1-4	:	The first four kings up to Artaxerxes, allusion to the starting point of the 70 weeks, and the 2300 evenings and mornings.
B	Dan. 11:5-39	:	Time covered by the little horn (after Rome up to the time of the end).
C	Dan. 11:40-45	:	At the time of the end (note vv. 40 and 45).
C_1	Dan. 12:1-4	:	At the time of the end (note vv. 1a and 1b: same time as in Dan. 11:45; cf. 12:4).

B_1	Dan. 12:5-11	:	Time covered by the little horn, reference made to a time and times and half a time (cf. 7:25) and to the 1290 days.
A_1	Dan. 12:12-13	:	Makes reference to the point of issue of the 2300 evenings and mornings in terms of "time of waiting" (this confirms once more the validity of the relationship between the prophecy of the 70 weeks and that of the 2300 evenings and mornings).

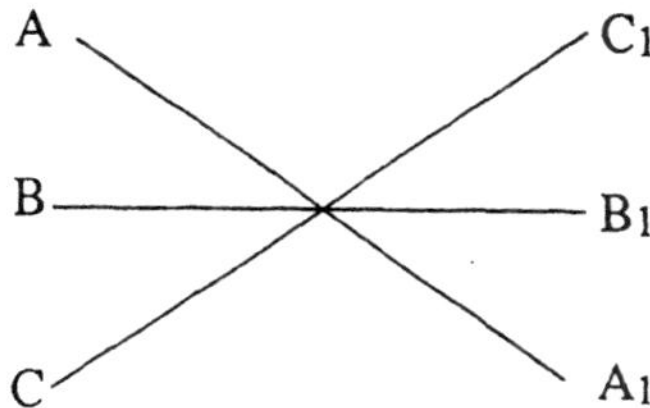

In brief, the power of the North has the same character and the same behavior as the little horn. The power of the North has the same destiny and the same end as the little horn. This power also covers the same period of time as the little horn. There is only one possible conclusion: the power of the North and the little horn are one and the same.[150]

It now remains for us to understand the nature of the conflict in which this power is engaged.

The North-South Conflict

A careful examination of the passage dealing with the conflict (Daniel 11:5-45) reveals two particular features throughout the text, namely the literary structure which molds it, and the constant reference to North and South. These two features are important, as they carry the key to the interpretation of the text which contains them.

The Literary Structure

The conflict between the North and the South starts exactly at verse 5. From this point on, the narrative develops in six sections according to a parallelism which establishes the relationship between the first three sections (vv. 5-12: A B C) and the next three (vv. 13-39: $A_1B_1C_1$);[151] verses 40-45 stand alone as a postscript, and are not paralleled within chapter 11, indicating thereby a new step in the course of the chapter.

A	The South with great dominion, v. 5. *rab* (great), v. 5 Frustrated alliances on the initiative of the South, between the South and the North, v. 6. *baṯ* (daughter), v. 6 A successor of the South appears in its place and enters the fortresses, vv. 7, 8. *w*^{e} *ʿāmad kannô* (appears in his place, fortress), v.7	A_1	The North with great army vv. 13-16. *rab* (great), vv. 13,14 Frustrated alliances on the initiative of the North, between the North and the South, v. 17 *baṯ* (daughter), v. 17 A successor of the North appears in its place and settles down in the fortresses, vv. 18-25a. *w*^{e} *ʿāmad kannô* (appears in his place, fortress), vv. 20,21
B	The North attacks the South with a great army and retreats to his own land, vv. 9, 10. *w*^{e}*šaḇ ʾel- admatô* (retreats to his own land), v. 9	B_1	The South attacks the North with a great army and retreats to his own land, vv. 25b-28. *w*^{e}*yašob ʾarṣo* (retreats to his own land), v. 28

C The South attacks the North, the king's pride, vv. 11, 12.
w^{e}*he ʿemîd . . . w*^{e}*nittan* (they will rise in rebellion . . . and will give), v. 11
y^{e}*rōm l*^{e}*ḇaḇo* (his heart shall be exalted), v. 12

C_1 The North attacks the South, the king's pride, vv. 29-39.
yaʿ^{a}*mōdû . . . w*^{e}*nātnû* (they will rise in rebellion . . . and will give), v. 31
w^{e}*yiṯrômēm* (he shall exalt himself), v. 36

D Postscript: Time of the end in four phases (vv. 40-45):

1. South and North attack each other (South against North, North against South) v. 40

2. Four movements of the King of the North

   North ——→ South v. 41a
   South ——→ North (following the geographical movement S-N Edom, Moab, Ammon) v. 41b
   North ——→ South vv. 42-43
   South ——→ North v. 44

3. North and South together (v. 43b) against the holy mountain (last stop) v. 45a

4. Kingdom of God implied in the phrase: "he shall come to his end without help" v. 45b

The analysis of the structure of this passage calls for a number of observations:[152]

1. For the parallelism of ABC // $A_1B_1C_1$

a. We are dealing here with a parallelism which displays clearly delineated sections that refer to each other throughout the passage in themes, thoughts, words and expressions.

b. The aggressions from the North and the South take place according to an alternate movement:

A	aggression from the South
B	aggression from the North
C	aggression from the South
A_1	aggression from the North
B_1	aggression from the South
C_1	aggression from the North

c. When A deals with the South, conversely B deals with the North and inversely.

2. For the postscript D

a. Here also the North-South aggressors follow an alternate movement in a regular manner (v. 40).

b. The movements of the King of the North follow a regular pattern back and forth, up to the fourth trip.[153]

This feature of regularity and of coincidence on the literary level, provides the key to the interpretation of our passage: Daniel 11:5-45 does not lend to a strict literal interpretation; historical events may well be implied here, yet the deciphering of those references must also take into account the "spiritual" dimension the author tries to introduce in his description.[154] We are thus in the presence of a literary device, of a way of speaking destined to suggest happenings beyond the mere historical events as a philosophy of history. The point here is not so much the events *per se*, but the principle of a dramatic conflict between North and South.

The North-South Reference

Since the conflict is not to be interpreted on a literal level it thus appears that the two powers concerned must be interpreted in a spiritual sense. The key to the interpretation of Daniel 11:5-39 is therefore not exactly the same as that of vv. 1-4. The introduction is to be interpreted on the literal level whereas the body of the text, the conflict itself, is to be interpreted on the spiritual level.

Two reasons can be given to explain this phenomenon of hermeneutical shifting, which may appear as an inconsistency.

1. The prophecy of Daniel 11:1-4 is concerned with a period which is still part of the history of Daniel. The kingdoms concerned can be mentioned by name, that is, Persia and Jawan (the old name of Greece, see Joel 4:6; Zech. 9:13).

2. The last, but not least, reason is of a literary nature. It is obvious that as far as form and substance are concerned, Daniel 11:1-4 is clearly marked off from the rest of the passage. From the point of view of structure as well as thought, these four verses belong rather to the material of chapter 10. Not only the similarity of wording between chapter 11:1-2 and 10:20, 21 allows this connection,[155] but Dan. 11:1-4 also moves along the same line as Dan. 10, dealing with the same motif of war between Persia and Greece. On the other hand, from v. 5 on, the conflict is no more involving two specified historical powers such as Persia and Greece; the text deals now with two unidentified, symbolical powers, namely North and South.

The spiritual interpretation of the reference to the North and to the South is also attested in the Bible where the concept of the two powers conveys a specific spiritual meaning. In prophetic language the concept of the North is associated with the evil power which claims the place of God. It is from the North that the prophet Daniel sees the little horn coming. The northern origin of the little horn has already been suggested in Daniel 8:9. Thus the fact that the little horn expands towards the South, the East and the West implies a northern origin, the only direction omitted. The same allusive language is used in Daniel 8:4; the ram pushes westward, and northward and southward, implying the eastern origin of the ram which indeed represents the eastern kingdom of Media Persia (Daniel 8:20). This pointing to the Northern origin of the little horn may also support the interpretation according to which the expression "one of them" must refer to one of "the four winds of heaven" rather than to one of the horns (see our treatment of this verse above). The point which the biblical author makes is that the little horn comes from the North. The reason for this emphasis is that traditionally in Israel the sworn enemy, Babylon,[156] appears from the North (Is. 41:25; Ezek. 26:7; Zech. 2:6,7).

Moreover the concept of the North in itself conveys in Ancient Middle East mythology a meaningful religious reference. The North is the seat of the Canaanite god, Baal.[157] This shows to what extent the reference to the North, whether it alludes of the power of Babylon or the throne of Baal, is, for the Hebrews of those days, full of religious meaning and of a claim to divinity.

The prophet Isaiah specifically testifies to this line of thought:

> You said in your heart, I will ascend to heaven; above the stars of God; I will set my throne on high; I will sit on the mount of assembly in the far north; I will ascend above the heights of the clouds, I will make myself *like the Most High.*
>
> (Is. 14:13, 14, RSV; emphasis supplied)

On the other hand, the South, in biblical tradition symbolizes man's government without God. Specifically, it reminds us of the country of Egypt (cf. Daniel 11:43)[158] and the denials of God by its Pharaohs (cf. Ex. 5:2). Likewise, the mention of Egypt will later be associated with the security of man's government (cf. 2 Kings 18:21; Jer. 2:18; Is. 31:3).

Just as the idea of the North portrays a religious movement which raises itself to the level of God in order to take His place, so the idea of the South conveys the concept of a *human* movement which ignores God and relies on itself.[159]

To be sure, the entire meaning of this passage of Daniel 11 has not yet been exhausted. What we have been able to draw from it so far should not be taken as definitive and dogmatic conclusions; only directions are outlined here. It remains for us to go back into the text and construe it along new perspectives. Yet this task is not necessary for our purpose. The situation in time of the conflict, the literary structure, and the way North and South are referred to in Daniel 11, convey enough indications to invite a spiritual interpretation.

A Spiritual Interpretation

The structure of the passage clearly indicates two phases. The first phase (11:5-39) covers a period which parallels the struggles and activities of the little horn in 8:23-25. The second phase (11:40-45) covers a period which is called by the same expression as "the time of the end" in both Dan. 8 and Dan. 11 (8:14, 26; cf. 11:40), thereby indicating that we are dealing with the same period. Although the two sections are well delineated, the spiritual interpretation holds for the first phase as well as for the second one.

The First Phase (11:5-39)

Besides the lesson we learn from the literary features of the passage, the fact that this section is concerned with the little horn of Dan. 8 indicates that its material has to be interpreted on a spiritual level. It is significant indeed that consistently throughout the book of Daniel this power has been referred to in a spiritual manner. In Dan. 2 it is the clay, a different material, symbolically pointing to the human nature (2:41, 43); in Dan. 7 it is the little horn with human features (7:8; cf. 8:11). We know that this allusion to the "human" by Daniel conveys a spiritual connotation.

Moreover if we assume a spiritual interpretation for the second phase, as do most commentators,[160] we must be consistent and hold the same view for the preceding passage. Not only does the second section use the same poetic language of regularity and symmetry by reference to the king of the North and the king of the South, but the North of the preceding passages is implicitly referred to in the postscript by "the king of the South shall attack *him*" (Dan 11:40a; emphasis supplied). It follows then that the North-South reference should apply to the same thing before v. 40 as well as afterwards, hence in the whole of chapter 11.

Furthermore, the fact that this process evolves in 7 steps, the seventh one characterizing the time of the end, may also suggest a qualitative understanding of this number. This rhetorical device may then raise the question whether the sequence 1 to 7 follows a chronological order, or is to be understood "spiritually" as only expressing the abstract principle of the conflict. Although the second section of the first phase $A_1B_1C_1$ parallels the first one, ABC, suggesting that the action comes at the same time, we notice a new element in the second section which is completely absent in the first one. From A_1 on, the North-South war is regularly accompanied with an opposition to the people of God[161] (vv. 16, 17, 20,[162] 27, 30-36). This new element indicates a new step in the process and therefore suggests a progression. It is also noteworthy that this opposition against God's people follows the regular pattern (North-South/South-North/North-South) and recurs at every step. Thus, this opposition is shared by both powers implying a new relationship between them. From A_1 on, North and South are both *against* the people of God. It is also noteworthy that this opposition is twice put in the perspective of the end, once in connection to the South (vv. 27, 28), and once in connection to the North (v. 35).

The interpretation of this intricate passage is not easy. At this stage, the message we could at least decipher in Dan. 11:5-39 is the announcement of a bringing together of two "spiritual" forces, one, Babel of a religious nature, usurping God's power, and the other, Egypt of a secular and political essence. This interpretation is, by the way, supported by the vision of Dan. 2 which also describes the period coming after Rome, i.e., the same period, in terms of clay (a religious power) and of iron (a secular and political power). This bringing together is apparent with the North-South fight but also with their common opposition to God's people in the perspective of the end. This spiritual interpretation would not necessarily exclude a chronological process; the apparition of a new element from A_1 on, suggests a new step, hence a historical progression with an eschatological orientation.

Thus, the lesson is not only theological. The prophecy points here to a real historical event which also happens to contain a spiritual meaning with regard to the "time of the end." In other words, the event is historical in nature and eschatological in perspective, therefore preparing for the next phase.

The Second Phase (11:40-45)

The spiritual nature of the event described in these verses is suggested through the regularity involving the movements of the king of the North and the king of the South; it is also supported by the spiritual language pointing to mythical enemies of Israel "which have perished long since."[163] Furthermore, the reference to the extreme North (Ammon),[164] and the extreme south (Ethiopia) indicates that the author means the totality of the world,[165] and therefore speaks with a spiritual meaning. Indeed the section deals with a period called "time of the end," thus implying the spiritual meaning this expression already conveyed in Dan. 8. The progression of the event is clearly indicated. The movement evolves in three steps:

1. The prophecy tells us first that in the days of the end the king of the South and the king of the North will fight and overcome each other alternately in four back-and-forth movements leading ultimately to the victory of the king of the North over the king of the South.

- The South to the North (v. 40). Notice the sober mention of this attack.

- The North to the South (vv. 40-41a). Notice here, *by contrast* to the preceding campaign, the stylistic emphasis put on the active power of the king of the North. He shall come against the South equipped with a triple power "like a whirlwind, with chariots, and with many ships," and moving with a triple efficiency "he shall enter the countries, overwhelm them, and pass through." The meaning of this emphasis is to prepare for the final victory of the North over the South. After this introduction, designed to present the power of the North, his first campaign is indicated by "he will enter the glorious land and overthrow many countries" (v. 41a).

- The South to the North (v. 41b). The order in which the countries Edom-Moab-Ammon are mentioned suggests the South-North movement;[166] since these three countries escaped destruction, it implies a victory of the South over the North.

- The North to the South (vv. 42-43). In the same way as in the preceding movement, here also the order in which the countries Egypt-Libya-Ethiopia are mentioned suggests the North-South movement and implies the total victory of the North over the South. The fact that this time there is no escape,[167] *in contrast* to the preceding campaign where there was, indicates that this time all the countries[168] (including Edom, Moab, Ammon) have been overthrown. Indeed, the spiritual nature of this victory is intended since the North is said to have power over gold, silver and precious things. In Daniel's language this means power of a religious kind over his God (see esp. 11:8).[169] In other words, spiritually speaking, the South recognizes the North as a "divine" ruler.

2. Then, the text tells us that the South walks on "the heels of the North" (v. 43), following him, not only indicating the dynamic presence of the South with the North, but also again suggesting that the South has accepted the sovereignty and the leadership of the North. For the first time, North and South are together. This unique and final alliance, which was only tentative before (vv. 6, 17), has finally worked as they prepared to attack the holy

mountain, just as the section $A_1B_1C_1$ had already implicitly announced (see above).

From the extreme South, Ethiopia (v. 43b), the king of the North hears "news from the east and the north." From there the geography suggests that east and north is somewhere in Palestine, and this identification is confirmed by the very fact that the king of the North goes to that place. Indeed his final destination is the glorious holy mountain (v. 45a), i.e., in biblical language, Mount Zion.[170] His intention is obvious. Verse 44 told us that the king of the North went out with "great fury to destroy and annihilate many" (cf. 11:33; 12:2-3), and "many" (*rabîm*) indicates the people of God.[171]

3. Finally, in a third step (11:45b), the power of the North will meet its end "with no one to help him," an expression which implies the impending and sudden advent of God's kingdom (cf. Daniel 2:44, 45; 8:25).

Thus the prophetic vision of Daniel 11:40-45 reveals a battle of gigantic proportions in the last stage of human history,[172] rallying all the political and religious forces of the world under the same banner[173] against God and His saints, a battle which will end with God's victory.

Certainly the prophet of Revelation 16 has Daniel 11 in mind when dealing with what he calls the war of Armageddon. Indeed, several items in this prophecy indicate that Daniel 11 and Revelation 16 point to the same event.[174]

It is the same enemy, Babel. He is the one who persecutes the saints (Rev. 16:6) and blasphemes the name of God (16:9). Moreover Babel is explicitly mentioned at the end of the battle when its defeat is announced (Rev. 16:19). It is also implicitly referred to at the beginning of the battle when the author mentions the drying up of the river Euphrates, the event that prepared the fall of the historical Babel (Rev. 16:12).[175]

It is the same movement of "great gathering." As in Daniel 11, which tells about the gathering of all the powers of the North and South, the prophecy of Revelation 16 points to the gathering of "the kings of the earth, of the whole world" (16:14). No wonder then, that the prophet uses the name Armageddon to designate the last convulsions of human history. Armageddon means "the mount of the gathering."[176] This Hebrew word expresses the great gathering of the powers of the world, a meaning which fits the context of Revelation 16 (cf. vv. 14, 16) perfectly. Moreover, the figure of Babel, which plays an important role here, is also conveyed by the Hebrew phrase Armageddon, "mount of gathering." The only other biblical passage using it is Is. 14:13-14, which indeed portrays the usurpation by Babel. The fact that Revelation 16 refers to Isaiah 14 constitutes another connection with Daniel 11, which also has the latter in its background. Both Dan. 11 and Is. 14 speak of a power which relates itself to the North (see above, p. 86).

Armageddon reminds us, by association, of the ambition of Babel to sit on the throne of God, above the stars, on the mount of the gathering (Armageddon).

Moreover, the motif of "mount" and the expression "the farther sides of the north" in Is. 14:13, 14 convey a specific association of ideas which undoubtedly points to Mount Zion.[177] As Jon D. Levenson notices: "The expression *yarkete zapon* 'the utmost peak of Zaphon' appears in Ps. 48:3 as an epithet of Mount Zion, the whole expression being in synonymous parallelism with 'the city of the great king.' . . . In that event, Zion would also be perceived as reaching into the highest heavens, above the clouds and the stars."[178] Now the passage of Revelation 16 makes sense while confirming the vision of Daniel 11:45. All the gathering for the last battle will take place at "the glorious Holy Mountain." If the reference to Isaiah 14 is correct, this mountain is nothing but the "heavenly" Mount Zion.

Lastly, it is the same end which comes from above to the same power (Babylon in Rev. 16 as the North in Dan. 11).

The Issue at Stake

It clearly appears now that Daniel 11 and Revelation 16 are dealing with the same event.[179] We are therefore allowed to take both passages into consideration when examining the questions concerning the essence of that war.

Two Truths

In Daniel 11 we learn that for the last battle Babel will gather all the powers against the "glorious Holy Mountain" (Daniel 11:45). The same language occurs in the dream of the statue in Daniel 2 where the alliances of the kings are set up in the perspective of the mountain, which represents the Kingdom of God (Daniel 2:35, 45).

In Revelation 16, the last conflict is described in terms reminding one of the "historical" battle of Babel, thus suggesting a parallel between the two conflicts. Just as the drying up of the Euphrates had formerly led to the confrontation between Babel and the king of the East, so ultimately, Armageddon is the opposition between the mystic Babel and the God above, or more precisely, the coming of God. For it is not so much God Himself that the forces of Babel oppose. The battle is not of a philosophical nature, a kind of seminar where atheist and religious debaters might dispute. What stirs and bothers the camp of Babel is, above all, the threat of the coming of God. Actually, the gathering of the forces is organized with the prospect of the Great Day of God in mind.

The exceptional use of the biblical expression[180] "the battle of the Great Day of God" puts the emphasis on His coming. This battle is not simply a "battle of God" among others in Israel's history (cf. 2 Chron. 20:15; 1 Sam. 17:47). This battle concerns the Great Day of God; it is the absolute and decisive battle where the coming of the Kingdom of God is at stake. In fact, the next verse implies this reference as it depicts the other camp opposing Babel, longing for His coming and watching: "Behold, I am coming as a thief. Blessed is he who watches . . ." (Rev. 16:15).

In the last conflict, the enemy is not only concerned with the Kingdom of God; in Daniel 11 as in Revelation 16, the camp of the enemy is also identified as being opposed to the law of God, and more specifically to the Sabbath. This is suggested in Daniel 11 through the description of the power of the North "exalting and magnifying himself above every God" (v. 36), and "replacing the God of the fathers by a foreign God" (vv. 37, 38). This is explicitly indicated in the opening of Revelation 16, when "the first bowl of the wrath of God" is poured out; the enemies are identified as "the men who had the mark of the beast and those who worshiped his image" (v. 2). The wording of this denunciation points to Rev. 14:9, and thereby reveals that the other issue at stake in the impending Armageddon has to do with what we have interpreted as a reference to the Sabbath.

Thus, between the first and the sixth bowls, which lead to the battle of Armageddon, the enemy is described as standing not only against the commandment of the Sabbath, but also against the coming of the Kingdom of God. Indeed, *Sabbath keeping, which implies faith in Creation, and hope in the kingdom of God belong to the same struggle against Babel.*

In fact, the two "truths" point to the same rationale and are closely related to each other. To venture to believe in the restoration of the Kingdom of God, one must dare to believe in Creation, for the God who was able to raise the world from nothingness will also be able to recreate it from chaos.

Hope is a vision of the future which, paradoxically, is channeled through our memories. As we remember the event of Creation, we can think of the event of Recreation. Therefore, we can hope. "The fact that God is the Creator of the world means that He compasses the complete time process, ruling, determining and completing all ages."[181] Since God's work has been from the beginning, one may expect the end to also depend on Him.

It is significant that the "new earth," the event of hope *par excellence*, is announced in terms of Creation.

> For behold, I create new heavens and a new earth.
> (Is. 65:17; cf. Is. 66:22)

> And I saw a new heaven and a new earth, for the first heaven and the first earth had passed away, . . . Then I, John, saw the holy city, New Jerusalem, coming down out of heaven from God . . . .
> (Rev. 21:1, 2)

God is at the beginning and at the end of everything. He is "the Alpha and the Omega, the Beginning and the End" (Rev. 22:13; cf. 1:8).

No wonder this lesson is registered in the time of the last pulsation of human history. It is the very issue which underlies the ultimate conflict of Armageddon. Actually, all the dynamics of biblical faith concentrate on this acute consciousness of a God who is effectively present at the two extremities of history.

The Frame of the Bible

It is no accident that the Bible is literally framed with this double reference to the beginning and the end. Whether one turns to the Hebrew Bible (Gen. 1-2 to Mal. 3 or to 2 Chron. 36:21-23)[182] or to the two testaments of the standard Bible (Gen. 1:1 to Rev. 22:17-21), the Canon starts with a reference to Creation and closes with a reference to the hope for the Kingdom of God.

It is also noteworthy that this particular way of introducing and concluding is repeated within the Bible. John probably had this principle in mind when he introduced his gospel[183] with the miracle of Creation (John 1) and concluded Revelation with a calling for the coming Kingdom (Rev. 22:17-21). Similarly, the Pentateuch begins with Creation (Gen. 1 and 2) and ends with the hope of resurrection (Deut. 34:6; cf. Jude 9) and the prospect of the Promised Land (Deut. 34:1-3). This can also be seen in the book of Isaiah which starts with a reference to Creation (1:2) and ends with the hope of the Kingdom of God (Is. 66:22-23).

That the text begins with Creation and ends with the hope of the Kingdom is particularly significant in regard to the very message it intends to convey. In biblical literature the introduction and conclusion are commonly used as landmarks. Through their relationship they point to the central idea of the text that they enclose, as in a frame.[184]

Would it be going too far, then, to state that the central message of the *whole* Bible is contained in the fact that the Bible begins with Creation and ends with the Hope in the Kingdom of God? The biblical scholar, Claus Westermann, suggests this conclusion. In his booklet *Beginning and End in the Bible*, he observes, "In its first pages the Bible speaks of the beginning, and in its last pages, of the end. . . ." Therefore, he concludes that "the beginning and the end" are "the framework for the history of salvation" which is "the center of the Bible" and thereby it "takes on a new aspect which is essential for the Bible as a whole."[185]

From a very different perspective, the Jewish exegete and philosopher André Neher makes the same observation: "The first page of the Biblical canon is the story of the Creation (Gen. 1); that introduction to the world is a beginning, and Creation is the starting point of history. The last prophecy of the Old Testament, that of Malachi, is still to be found at the end of the collection of the prophets, and his words are those of the last of the canonical prophets. Time is fulfilled by the coming of God (Mal. 3:23ff.)." This literary phenomenon leads Neher to conclude that here "is embedded the very nature of Biblical things."[186]

Since the Bible begins with Creation and ends with the Kingdom of God, it follows that its central theme lies here in these two truths. This particular way of expression and thinking is explicitly attested to in one particular biblical passage, the Hymn of Faith in Hebrews 11.

It starts with Creation:

> By faith we understand that the worlds were framed by the word of God, so that the things which are seen were not made of things which are visible.
> (Heb. 11:3)

It ends with the Hope in the Kingdom:

> And all these, having obtained a good testimony through faith, did not receive the promise, God having provided something better for us, that they should not be made perfect apart from us.
> (Heb. 11:39, 40)

This literary procedure has also been noticed by S. Spicq, one of the most prominent experts on the epistle of Hebrews. He writes, "This chapter which had started with Creation, wonderfully ends with the discrete evocation of the final completion of humanity."[187]

Considering the importance given to the structure in the epistle of Hebrews,[188] we cannot help inferring that, by this means, the author is intending to point out the key idea of the passage, namely Creation and Hope in the Kingdom of God.

It is indeed significant that in the prelude to the poem, the author gives a definition of faith in which the same thoughts are associated.

> Now faith is the substance of things hoped for, the evidence of things not seen.
>
> (Heb. 11:1)

The "things not *seen*" (*blepomenon*) of v. 1 points to the "things which are *seen*" (*blepomenon*) in v. 3, referring to the act of Creation. The "things hoped for" of v. 1 points to the promised kingdom of v. 39.

This poetic meditation on faith coming from within the Scriptures substantiates our view with regard to the principle which sustains the whole Bible. The only definition of faith we find in the Bible meets the criterion which is suggested when the Bible is taken as a whole. *Though it may be considered as a mere point of doctrine—Creation and God's Kingdom—it is the whole biblical revelation which is at stake in the preparation for the Battle of Armageddon.*

The camp of God defines itself as a faith which "stubbornly" persists in believing in Creation, and as a hope which expects only the heavenly Kingdom. On the opposite side stands the camp of Babel, involved in the frenzied enterprise of usurping God's place, making the genius from below its own creator and end, its alpha and omega.

* * * *

The revelations of biblical prophecy converge to define this time as "the time of the end." This is a time which has been dated by the prophet, starting in 1844. In the beginning of this chapter we asked the question about the reason for this date. Indeed, the question is legitimate. The event which is seen by the prophet is supposed to take place in heaven, i.e., beyond any kind of control whatsoever; it is therefore important to have some clues from our human history which could provide the necessary reference for this observation. Actually the prophet does indicate a corresponding event on earth. Parallel to the heavenly *kippur* the prophecy points to the rise of two distinct movements on earth which happen to characterize the historical period of 1844:

1. On one hand it is a time when mankind rejects the idea of Creation and of the Kingdom of above, to promote, instead, the idea of evolution.[189] It is a time which promotes the beginning of movements of unity[190] involving the international scene for the first time.

2. On the other hand it is a time that witnesses a renewed recollection of Creation and the announcement of a judgment, a time of waiting and hoping.[191] Indeed, the 19th century perfectly fits the prophetic description. Would it be correct, then, if we inferred from this observation that the prophecy indeed has been fulfilled? This would mean that we are provided here below with some control, hence with a reason for this peculiar date (1844). These movements, which started then and are still active today, might be considered in human history as symptoms of the preparation for the heavenly Kingdom.

CHAPTER FOUR

THE VISION OF MICHAEL

"At that time Michael shall stand up."
Daniel 12:1

The last event in Daniel's prophecy deserves a particular treatment. The whole book of Daniel points to it; needless to say, it contains the most important message of the prophet. Significantly, the book of Daniel does not concentrate its references to this event to a single passage as is the case for the three other aspects of the end, Judgment (ch. 7), Waiting (ch. 12), and War (ch. 11). The passages dealing with the event of the Kingdom are scattered throughout the book of Daniel.

This last chapter will function as a kind of synthesis and eventually as the conclusion of our work. It was expected to be so since the event of the Kingdom, in essence, not only reviews and synthesizes all the trends of the book but also marks the end. In addition to that, beyond the exegetical task, the prophecy requires now more than just an academic assignment. It calls for an existential reflection. It is not usual that a book with scholarly purpose would also include a "spiritual" meditation. Yet, this is not a digression; the book of Daniel appeals to that effort. More than just historical information or a philosophical insight, it conveys hope for our human anguish.

Up to now, the mention of Michael was strictly indirect. Never has the prophet seen Michael in a vision, or if he saw him, he did not or could not identify him. It is the Son of God in Dan. 3 or the angel in Dan. 6, the Son of Man in Dan. 7, the Prince of the host or the Prince of Princes in Dan. 8, the Prince in Dan. 9:26a, the man clothed in linen in Dan. 10 (cf. 12). Whenever Michael was identified He was just referred to by a third person as someone who helped in the battle (10:13, 21). For the first time Michael is now seen in the vision. It is, then, a vision of victory, a vision of hope.

The vision of Michael is portrayed against a background of hopelessness. Just preceding the mention of Michael, the last verse was full of death and indicated a tragic end. "He shall come to his end, and no one will help him" (Daniel 11:45). Also, the time of the advent of Michael is depicted as "a time of trouble such as never was since there was a nation" (Daniel 12:1). This shows how great the surprise of this salvation will be. In this context the name of Michael plays its semantic function. *Mi-ka-el* means "who is like God!" In biblical tradition this interjection expresses the intensity of human awe towards God's unexpected victory (Ex. 15:11-12). This expression is generally used in connection with a war.[192] In our context, this connotation is also further supported by the Hebrew verb which accompanies the mention of Michael *'āmad* (to stand up, arise). Chapter 11 contains twelve occurences of this verb, all of them in relation to the victory of a king who takes rule. The verb *'āmad* is used here with Michael, the last king to achieve His victory and take His rule.

It is also noteworthy that the "standing up of Michael" in the beginning of chapter 12 of Daniel is repeated at the end of the chapter by the "standing up of man," the resurrection of Daniel. The same Hebrew word *'āmad* is used to designate both events. God's victory brings Daniel's victory.

God's Victory

"Michael shall stand up," Daniel 12:1. The God who speaks such words is not the God of idealistic dreamers. He is, first of all, a God of action who will come and surprise the world; He will surprise by the reality and violence of His coming.

The Violence of God

The coming of Michael involves violence. It is inevitable. Whenever God crosses the way of man, whether it be in Israel, in human history, or even in our personal lives, it always means a shock, a disrupting violence. The book of Daniel in particular tells us about this violence of God operating in the course of history.

Violence in History

The book of Daniel begins with this theme of violence. The Lord gave Israel into the hand of Nebuchadnezzar (1:1-2). "God is the one who removes kings and raises up kings" (2:21); He makes Nebuchadnezzar like an animal (ch. 4) and causes the fall of Belshazzar (ch. 5). He fights against the nations (10:13, 21). Daniel himself is affected by this violence (10:8, 9).

God's violence is also manifest when He breaks the rules of nature. Wisdom is imparted at His will (2:21) ignoring the natural process of learning and training; in ten days the Hebrews become ten times wiser than the professionals (1:20). God penetrates into the minds of kings as well as of prophets; He imposes His revelations through their dreams and visions in spite of their conscious will (ch. 2; 7-12). The animal is made to stand on two feet, and a man's heart is implanted in it (7:4; 4:33-37). The fire of the furnace does not burn (ch. 3), and the hungry lions do not devour (ch. 6). Yet the course of history keeps flowing and these incursions from above are only furtive and incomplete.

Violence at the End of History

What will it be like at the end of History, when God Himself will "stand up" and take everything into His hands? In chapter 2 Daniel compares the coming of the Kingdom of God to a stone which is thrown and crushes all the earthly kingdoms (2:35, 45). In chapter 7 the Kingdom of God goes along with "taking away, consuming and destroying" (7:26). Chapter 8 describes the coming of the Kingdom of God in terms of "breaking" (8:25b). Finally, chapter 11 describes the sudden interruption of all the busy preparations of the earthly kingdoms by a simple, yet very suggestive "and he shall come to his end" (11:45). These last words were not expected, inasmuch as all powers seemed well prepared to accomplish their own objectives. The surprise and violence are always the same characteristic features of this last coming of God.

Violence of Love

God's love requires it. Paradoxically, it is because God loves that He shakes. Love cannot work and save without the violence of His intervention. The writers of the Psalms, from the pit of their misery, so well understood this requirement that they did not hesitate to identify their Savior as the avenging God; Ps. 94 is an example of that kind:

> O Lord God, to whom vengeance belongs
> God, to whom vengeance belongs, shine forth!
> Rise up, O Judge of the earth;
> Render punishment to the proud.
> Lord, *how long* will the wicked,
> *How long* will the wicked triumph?
> (Ps. 94:1-3)

All these Psalms play on the same theme, the final day of the coming of God. The violence of God is identified with redemption. The *Goel* (the avenger) is both the one who saves and the one who avenges (cf. Ps. 119:154; 77:14-16; 18:46-47; etc.). The "how long" questions of the Psalms (e.g. Ps. 6:3; 74:10; 80:4; 82:2; 90:13; etc.) are dramatically echoed in the book of Daniel in connection with the agony of the saints and the coming of the final deliverance (Daniel 8:13; 12:6).

The "how long?" of the Psalms and Daniel does not expect an answer prompted by either demagoguery or good will. The "how long?" is cried out with clenched fists and teeth and expects the true liberation, the radical revolution, the "change." The effective, physical coming of the God of above, of His Kingdom, the *other* kingdom, is indeed the only valid response to the poignant question of evil and suffering.

The Heavenly Kingdom

Actually, the violence of His coming has to do with His alien origin. When Daniel refers to God or to His Kingdom, he repeatedly speaks of heavenly events. The expression, "God of heaven," is the most frequently used phrase to characterize God in the book of Daniel, thereby referring to a God "whose dwelling is not with flesh" (2:11). Likewise, the Kingdom of God, which is supposed to come at the end of human history is set up by the God of heaven (2:44), and has nothing to do with man's initiative. This idea is forcefully pointed out through the repetitive formula which regularly marks the end of the earthly kingdom:

"a stone cut out without hands" (2:45)

"he shall be broken without hand" (8:25)

"he shall come to his end without help" (11:45)

Chapter 7 describes the coming of the Kingdom of God in terms of "the son of man coming with the clouds of heaven" (7:13).

The language is explicit enough to suggest a kingdom coming from "up there," a kingdom which is essentially different from the earthly kingdoms represented by beasts.

The fact that the heavenly kingdom is described by reference to the son of man in Daniel 7:13, 14, and by reference to the saints in Daniel 7:27 does not, however, allow "the assimilation of this people of Israelite Saints to divine stature."[193] Daniel 7:9-14 is about heaven and God, whereas Daniel 7:23-27 concerns itself with the earth and human beings. The association heaven-God belongs to the kingdom of the Son of man, whereas the association earth-humans belongs to the kingdom of the saints. The two sides are distinct but complementary (cf. Daniel 7:25). Likewise, when Daniel tells Nebuchadnezzar that he, as king, is the head of the statue, he does not mean that he *is* Babylon. Moreover, Daniel 12:1-2, which speaks of the coming of Michael in a way parallel to the coming of the Son of man in Daniel 7, clearly distinguishes Him from the people making up the saints. Michael is identified in the book of Daniel as a heavenly being, which not only points to the heavenly nature of the "holy mountain" involved in the context of His coming (11:45-12:1), but also clarifies the other reference to "the mountain" in Daniel 2:35, 45. In both passages the mountain refers to the heavenly Zion. Indeed, the Kingdom of God belongs to another order.

This does not simply mean that the two attributes of this kingdom lie beyond our understanding (cf. 1 Cor. 2:9); it indicates the full reality of this promise. The kingdom does not come from us, a sort of hallucination or poetic dream; it is an announced kingdom, an objective and palpable reality which comes from outside this earth at a precise moment in history. Moreover, it is the only kingdom which stands the test of time, the only one which is not transitory.

> His dominion is an everlasting dominion, which shall not pass away.
>
> (Daniel 7:14; cf. Daniel 2:44)

That presents a problem to many people. The idea of a heavenly kingdom is readily accepted and even meditated on as long as it remains in the spiritual sphere—a moral, a fiction, or a myth. We have a hard time getting used to the idea of a real place that is somewhere else and different, a place where we might actually live. Indeed, we are so used to this space, this life, that it is difficult for us to imagine another world. We are so comfortable at home, and so well adjusted to this world that it is inconceivable that something else could exist. That earthly city of humanity is so beautiful and so real that it cuts off the sight of God. People today no longer believe in the Kingdom of God. The less they believe, the greater the surprise will be.

Call for Wisdom

The coming of Michael from above requires those below to be prepared, or rather, if we follow Daniel's advice, "to be wise." Only "those who are wise shall shine" (12:3). Verse 1 had already made this point by referring back to the works of the Judgment: "Your people shall be delivered, everyone who is found written in the book" (12:1). Thus the coming of the Kingdom is related to the Judgment, and as Michael stands up, Judgment is brought to mind. The same process is described in Daniel 7:13-14 where the coming of the Son of Man is accompanied by a "flashback" to the Judgment. This is indicated in the tenses of the verbs used in this passage. Three phases are suggested:

Phase I is the "actual" time of His coming (verb in participle): the Parousia. "And behold one like the Son of Man *coming* with the clouds of heaven," v. 13a.

Phase II refers back to a time "before" His coming (verbs in perfect):[194] the Judgment. "He *had come* to the Ancient of Days and they *had brought* Him near before Him. Then to him *had been given* dominion and glory and a kingdom," v. 13b, 14a.

Phase III points to a future "after" His coming (verbs in imperfect): "And all peoples, nations, and languages *will serve* Him. His dominion an everlasting dominion, which *shall not pass away*, and His kingdom the one which *shall not be destroyed*," v. 14.

If Daniel 12, like Daniel 7, describes the coming of the Kingdom in connection with the past event of Judgment, it is not only because the Judgment prepares for the Kingdom of God as such, it is essentially to convey a specific lesson or warning: "be wise enough to be found in the book when He comes." To be sure, Daniel's understanding of wisdom is not necessarily what we may think it is. We are missing the point if we reduce this wisdom to "the good boy" who perfectly fits the social mold. That Daniel and the three Hebrews are also called "wise," which this passage of Daniel 12 repeats, is indicative of the intention of the author to suggest the kind of wisdom he has in mind. Daniel and the three Hebrews set the example.

Be Different!

The coming of the "God of heaven" implies an existence which harmonizes with this "other" kingdom—a "*different*" way of life.

Because biblical religion runs contrary to most human nature, it necessarily implies struggle and discipline in the rebellious course of daily life. "To be wise" requires, as with Daniel and the other three Hebrews, a specific training program which may even seem ridiculous and bizarre to the people in the city of Babel, who do not understand (cf. Daniel 1:10).

While waiting for the great day, the believer can hardly live like others. Even his eating and drinking are involved in the matter. This does not mean, however, that how he lives here will ensure him the inheritance of the Kingdom. Salvation is not achieved through works. Salvation is a gift through grace. The three Hebrews understood this as they decided to serve their Lord regardless of the results. Their response to the threat of the king ("if not . . ." 3:18) contains the whole biblical theology of grace. Their works were not aimed at salvation; instead they were the fruit of God's grace and therefore expressed their *gracious* faithfulness. The same rationale is apparent in Daniel's prayer as he asks God for salvation, not "because of our righteous deeds, but because of Your great mercies" (9:18). What triggers the process of conversion does not proceed from below, as in the worship or following of Babel, but from above, from the forthcoming event. The future determines the present and not the reverse. It is the certainty of the Kingdom which inspires works; it is not the eagerness to gain the Kingdom that should motivate believers.

Be Watchful!

In the expectation of God's visitation, Daniel keeps praying three times a day as he always did, with the window open toward Jerusalem (Daniel 6:10). Daniel keeps waiting until the end of his life (6:16). Likewise the three Hebrews are faithful until the end (3:23). The blessing attached to the "waiting" attitude is prolonged with "and come to . . ." (12:12). It is not enough to start the process of waiting. We must also remain there until "we come to. . . ." The warning has been sounded by the prophecy.

> Blessed is he who watches, and keeps his garments,
> lest he walk naked and they see his shame.
> (Rev. 16:15)

The alarm is given here to the believers who are waiting.[195] They must be persistant in their vigilance. Ridicule and shame await them every moment. Nothing is ever acquired permanently. The fact that you made your choice yesterday does not guarantee the future. Our text indicates, with humor and irony, that they would stroll about naked, while they firmly believe themselves to be dressed.[196] A call for awakening, for lucidity and constancy, the oracle cautions us about feeling as if we had arrived. The spirit of Babel can even infiltrate into the ranks of those who wait for Jerusalem.

Be Happy!

Furthermore, this particular expectation which appears at first to portray anguish and tension, sometimes denounced as a kind of psychosis, is instead related to happiness. "Blessed is he who waits" is the message of the book of Daniel (12:12). The ideal does not imply sorrow and sadness; on the contrary, it brings happiness and energy. The Hebrew word *'ašrēy* (blessed), which conveys the biblical idea of happiness, is etymologically related to the idea of "going forward" and "moving" (*'āšar*). This is true on the psychological level. A life without any expectation would be a meaningless and tasteless life. Indeed, happiness has nothing to do with what you are—a state, however nice it may be—or with what you have—possessions, however rich they may be. Happiness cannot be experienced except in the dynamics of expectation. Only the one who waits for something beyond his present status is happy, because there is then a reason to act and to move.

There is more here than just a lesson in psychology. The event which is looming on the horizon is not like other events. God is coming! And this means real happiness, happiness which has for so long been elusive and dreamed about.

Therefore, the heart bursts out, and we cannot keep the news to ourselves. We must share it. Because the news makes us happy, waiting is "contagious." Daniel did not confine himself to his own corner of piety. He reached out to the steward to justify his position and even tried to convince him with the argument of a test (1:12-14). He witnessed before kings (2:27-30), or urged them to repentance (4:27). Following his example those called "the people who understand" are described as making others understand (11:33). The use of the same word *bîn* (understand) specifically refers in the book of Daniel to the interpretation of the prophecy of the end (Daniel 8:15, 17, 27; 9:2, 22, 23; 12:8, 10). It shows that this "sharing" goes beyond the simple "alleluia," the beautiful testimony; it essentially has to do with the painful communication of this kind of material. He who waits cannot wait alone, especially because what he waits for concerns others.

Daniel's Victory

Another surprise accompanies the coming of God: the surprise of the dead who awake (Dan. 12:2) and "stand up" from the dust, astonished, for the grace of new life (Dan. 12:13).

The miracle of resurrection is not easy to conceive or to assume. Actually, resurrection is useless for those who refuse to think that death is total and believe in the immortality of the soul. Resurrection is irrational for those who accept death as total and conceive man as mere matter. The lesson which is registered in the book of Daniel is quite different from both views. There, resurrection is total, involving every aspect of the human being; resurrection is total because it implies total death, and death is total because it implies total life.

Total Life

Total life is life which embraces the entire being. This ideal is suggested in the book of Daniel because of its specific concept of the nature of man. Our heroes are characterized as "young men in whom there was no blemish, but good-looking, gifted in all wisdom, possessing knowledge and quick to understand" (1:4). Intellectual abilities as well as physical health and grace are taken into consideration. The human is conceived as a whole, encompassing intellectual, physical, and spiritual attributes. This conception is immediately confirmed by the ten-day test. Well nourished, the Hebrews become wiser than anyone else.

This ideal does not promote an "elitist" theory,[197] however. Nothing is solved at the mere level of humanity. The prolonging of Nebuchadnezzar's prosperity depended upon his "mercy to the poor" (4:27). Wisdom, knowledge, and skills and good health all come from God, and are the actual result of His gifts (1:17; 2:21). Thus to the modern psychosomatic concept,[198] the book of Daniel adds another perspective, namely the reference to religious and moral[199] dimensions. The "perfect" person then is the one who harmoniously combines all the physical, mental, moral and religious faculties.

Total life is founded upon the harmonious development of the whole person, body, mind and soul, with every mode of being related to the others and affecting the whole being. Total life is a life that involves the totality of human nature and recognizes the acute consciousness of its unity.

Total Death

The lesson implied with regard to death also involves every aspect of life. Body, mind and soul are doomed to death, and man disappears completely. *If man is one, his life like his death, will be total.* Great is the temptation to ignore the void and to refuse the end. In the book of Daniel, the pagan kings do not accept death. Nebuchadnezzar wants to be eternal and builds the statue entirely of gold (ch. 3). Belshazzar shows the same concern as he praises "the gods of silver and gold, bronze and iron . . ." (5:23). This association of metals pointing to the metals of the statue may well suggest that Belshazzar not only knows about the vision of the statue, but wants to control the stages that follow. In regard to Darius, a slight hint of the same preoccupation might be perceived through the allusion to the eternal character of his law (6:8, 12, 15). Ironically, the king is the prisoner of this eternity; he cannot change it (6:17). Besides the intention to prepare for the following miracle and to prevent the king from changing his mind, this irrevocable decree may also point to the royal claim for godship, in accordance with the content of the decree itself. All of these kings were greeted with the same wish for eternity, "O king, live forever" (2:4; 3:9; 6:21).

The temptation of immortality attracted the pagan kings who aspired to equal God himself. This ambition is explicitly denounced by Daniel in his prediction of an earthly king who will "exalt himself and magnify himself above every god" (11:36; cf. 8:11). Actually the former proposition implies the latter one: to declare man immortal means to raise man to God's level. But, as King Darius ultimately recognizes, only "*He*[200] is the living God and steadfast for ever" (6:26; cf. 4:34).

What King Darius understood at the end of his experience with the God of Daniel is emphasized throughout the book of Daniel. As we have already indicated, this book is pervaded with the prospect of the end. Israel's history has come to an end. The end of the earthly kingdoms is repeated over and over again. All of them are bound to return to dust. The only kingdom which will last is from above, the Kingdom of God. When Daniel happens to suggest a prolongation for Nebuchadnezzar's reign, it is just "a lengthening," which is even modified with a "perhaps" (4:27). Daniel himself is told by the angel that he has an end (12:13). In contrast to the pagan kings who flee the totality of their end, the Hebrews face it and do not resist the command to be cast into the pit (ch. 3 and 6). They know what they are: just dust. The traditional way that Daniel prayed, "with fasting, sackcloth, and ashes" (9:3) expresses this awareness concerning man's nature and destiny.[201] Man is "nothing" (4:34) and is doomed to "the dust of the earth" (12:2).

Total Wakening

To hope within such certainty is unreasonable. After death there is nothing left; yet the prophet keeps waiting, for he knows about the great miracle of the Resurrection. Daniel had been saved from the lions' den (ch. 6) and his three companions from the fire (ch. 3). He had witnessed the transforming of Nebuchadnezzar from a beastlike creature into a human being again. He can "conceive" the daring picture. The miracle is not just a dream generated from the need to be saved.[202] Daniel has experienced the power of Creation even in his own life.

No wonder that faith in Creation takes such an important place in Daniel's theology; indeed, the idea of Creation runs through the whole book of Daniel. The first time Daniel and his companions have to situate themselves in regard to their religion, they do it by reference to the Creator (1:12). God is defined in chapter 2 as the one "who changes the times and seasons" (2:21), an expression which points to His power as the Creator (cf. Gen. 1:4, 14). In Daniel 3 and 6 God acts as the Creator; He delivers the Hebrews from the pit of death. This miracle is interpreted by the King who witnesses it as a demonstration of God's power of Creation: "He is the living God. . . . He works signs and wonders in Heaven and on earth" (6:26, 27). Chapter 7 starts with an allusion to Creation. The language which conveys the appearance of the beasts coming up from the sea and out of the four winds of heaven is reminiscent of the Creation story (Gen 1:1, 20). Daniel 8 alludes to Creation through the expression "evenings and mornings" which points to Genesis 1, the only other biblical reference using such a phrase. The idea of Creation stands in the background of Daniel 9 where the event of Salvation is brought out in connection with the Jubilee, the Sabbath of Sabbaths.

This strong reference to Creation teaches us about the nature of hope, pointing to the process of salvation—a new Creation. In this perspective, death is no more a threat, just a sleep, for the miracle of Creation will work; "and many of those who *sleep* in the dust of the earth shall awake" (12:2). "You shall *rest* and will arise" (12:13).

Thus, God does not resort to any inventory of souls supposedly returned to heaven for manufacturing the new person. The operation is performed right there, in the dust. The lesson is important indeed. It not only teaches us about the state of the dead; it also reassures us about the recovery of our identity. The resurrected one is not another person; it is the same one who slept in the grave.

The resurrection concerns the whole human being, complete *with* his body. When he wakes up, the individual finds himself as he was before sleeping. Daniel's anthropology is consistent until the end. Man remains a whole from life to death, and from death to life.

But the miracle does not stop here. The resurrection is not a mere recovery to meet the nostalgia of one's lost past. This is not merely a return to life with the resumption of one's old activities. Where would hope be if the same maimed flesh and the same troubles were awaiting us? The awakening will carry with it the greatest surprise. From the heart to the blood, from the brain to the senses, we shall vibrate totally with a new life.

This process is indicated through the respective experiences of the Hebrews and Nebuchadnezzar. Out of the pit man emerges greater. Daniel and his three companions are promoted (6:28; 3:30), and "excellent majesty is added" to Nebuchadnezzar (4:36). Lastly, this transformation which will take place on the Day of Resurrection, is wonderfully described by the words of the angel: "Many of those who shall sleep in the dust . . . shall shine . . . like the stars" (12:2-3)—from dust, to stars.

To say that human beings out of dust "shall shine like stars," not only suggests the miracle of the resurrection process but also indicates the nature of the change. They will then possess life, the total life. Only on the great morning of the Resurrection will we understand; we will know then what it means to have total life (cf. 1 Cor. 13:12). Total life is barely sketched in today's shadow of existence—just enough to give us a taste of something else, just enough to nurture our dreams, and to hope, looking up "to the stars."

NOTES

[1]William Griffin, ed., *Endtime: The Doomsday Catalog*, 1979.

[2]See J. Doukhan, *Aux portes de l'Espérance*, 1983, pp. 29-43; cf. André Neher, *The Prophetic Existence*, 1969, p. 12; cf. Ed. Jacob, "Prêcher sur l'Ancien Testament," *RHPR* 61 (1981):333; cf. G. F. Hasel, "The Problem of the Center in the OT Theology Debate," *ZAW* 86 (1974):65-82. G. F. Hasel, *Old Testament Theology: Basic Issues in the Current Debate*, 1985, p. 142. Cf. T. C. Vriezen, *An Outline of Old Testament Theology*, 1970, p. 458. Cf. D. Baly, *God and History in the Old Testament*, 1976, p. 89. Cf. E. Sellin,

Theologie des AT, 1936, pp. 21-23. Cf. W. Zimmerli, "Promise and Fulfillment," in *Essays on Old Testament Hermeneutics*, ed. by C. Westermann, 1963, p. 112. Cf. G. Hasel, *Old Testament Theology*, 1985, p. 180.

[3]This observation holds with regard to the NT as well; if we count the number of occurrences of the motif of the end in the James Strong, *Exhaustive Concordance* including every rendering in the original, the number is still greater in the book of Daniel.

[4]See A. Lengler, "La structure littéraire de Daniel 2-7," *Bib* 53 (1972):169-190. Cf. Joyce Baldwin, *Daniel: An Introduction and Commentary*, 1978, pp. 57-62. Cf. W. H. Shea, "Unity of Daniel," in *Symposium on Daniel*, Frank B. Holbrook, ed., 1986, pp. 249-252.

[5]See W. H. Shea, ibid., and especially on the linguistic links between 8 and 11, see ibid., p. 246.

[6]These are the only two biblical passages which use the particular word *šāḇuʿîm* for weeks.

[7]Chapter one begins with the end (the exile) and closes with the end (end of the exile); furthermore, the motif of the end appears several times in the text (v. 5, 15, 18). It is also noteworthy that the last occurrence of this motif (v. 18) uses the expression "end of the days" which is only repeated in 12:13 where the same pattern of expression refers to the cosmic end of the world.

[8]Although verses 5-39 do not belong to the section directly dealing with "the time of the end" (see vv. 40-45), the fact that they describe the same fight between the King of the North and the King of the South just as in vv. 40-45 shows that vv. 5-39 are written from the same perspective of the end. The same remark holds for the feet of ch. 2 and the little horn of ch. 7 and 8; both entities are placed in the same section dealing with the end. This phenomenon may be explained by the fact that these entities represent a kingdom which happens to survive until the time of the end.

[9]See especially D. S. Russel, *The Method and Message of Jewish Apocalyptic*, 1964, p. 16.

[10]This thesis, already claimed by the neo-platonist Porphyry (233-304 A.D.) in his anti-Christian polemic, has been taken over by most modern critical scholars (cf. especially O. Plöger, *Das Buch Daniel*, 1965; F. Hartman and A. di Lella, *The Book of Daniel*, AB, 1977; A. Lacocque, *The Book of Daniel*, 1979, etc.). Five main arguments are usually set forth to support the second-century dating:

1. The book of Daniel belongs to the apocalyptic currents and therefore according to the evolutionist scheme of Hegel must come at the latest stage of the History of Israel (thesis: prophetic school, antithesis: priestly school, synthesis: apocalyptic school). This argument ignores the fact that a good number of apocalyptic texts have been written in other periods as well (cf. Gen. 3:15, Is. 24-27, and several passages in the books of Zechariah and Ezekiel).

2. In the Hebrew Bible, the book of Daniel has not been classified in the prophetic section as expected, but in the third and last section (Esther, Daniel, Ezra, Nehemiah, I-II Chronicles). Therefore, the book of Daniel should have been written after the prophets. This argument stumbles on the fact that this section contains other old writings such as Job, some Psalms, etc. Besides, this classification may as well have considered the specific style and content of the book of Daniel which make it closer in "genre" to the third category than to the so-called prophetic texts. For example, we do not have the classic introductory formula of the prophet "Thus spoke the Lord . . . ." It is moreover noteworthy that never in the book is Daniel designated as a prophet (*nabi*). In fact, the very root of this word is virtually absent in the book (only appearing in ch. 9:6, 10, 24, obviously referring here to other prophets than Daniel himself). On the other hand, Daniel is referred to as a wise man (cf. Dan. 1:17-21; 2:24-30). And this tradition may well have been conveyed by Ezekiel (cf. 28:3); if it is the case, this could have some important bearing upon the Daniel that Ezekiel is referring to, hence upon the question of the dating of this book. Daniel's tie to the sapiential tradition has been noted in Jewish tradition (cf. Malbim's commentary on Daniel,

Yefeach Laketz on ch. 1:4) as well as in modern commentators (cf. Lacocque, pp. 32-33; cf. G. von Rad, *Old Testament Theology*, 1965, p. 306ff.). Moreover, this book is imbued with historical and political events and denotes a philosophy of history which reminds us of the book of Chronicles (cf. R. J. Coggins, *The First and Second Books of Chronicles*, 1976, pp. 4ff.; cf. A. G. Welch, *The Work of the Chronicler*, 1939, pp. 53-54). The same "historico-eschatological" orientation underlies both books which end the same way, by reference to Cyrus (see 2 Ch. 36:22-23; cf. Dan. 10:1; cf. Dan. 1:21; see also the connection between 2 Ch. 36:21, 27 and Dan. 9:22.). This accent on both wisdom and history fits perfectly the personality of Daniel, who like Joseph holds the double function of wise man and statesman. (For the affinities between Joseph and Daniel, cf. Siracide 39:4, 18-19.)

3. The advanced angelology of the book of Daniel would plead on behalf of its late dating. A thorough analysis of the passages of the book dealing with angels shows, however, that they have much more affinity with books like Ezekiel and Zechariah of the 6th century B.C., than with the apocalyptic literature of the 2nd century B.C. (cf. A. C. Welch, *Visions of the End*, 1922, p. 129).

4. The argument of historical errors cannot be taken as a serious evidence for a late dating. Besides, these alleged errors are more and more contested and explained in the light of new historical data (cf. G. Archer, *Introduction*; cf. also W. Shea's articles in *AUSS* 9 [1971] and 10 [1972]).

5. As for the Greek words which are used in the book of Daniel for musical instruments, they are by no means convincing arguments for a late dating. It has been demonstrated that the Greek influence had been already at work in Babylon since the 7th century B.C., especially in the domain of fine arts and music (cf. W. F. Albright, *From the Stone Age to Christianity*, 1957, pp. 337ff.; E. M. Yamauchi, *Greece and Babylon*, 1967, p. 94; T. C. Mitchell and R. Joice, "The Musical Instruments in Nebuchadnezzar's Orchestra," in *Notes on Some Problems in the Book of Daniel*, 1965, p. 19-27).

If the arguments of the critics are questionable, on the other hand, we can easily justify the traditional dating of the 6th century

B.C. for the book of Daniel on the basis of at least five observations:

a. The way of dating the visions in the book of Daniel (cf. 2:1; 7:1; 8:1; 9:1; 10:1) is the same as in the books of Jeremiah and Ezekiel (cf. Jer. 1:3; 25:1, etc; Ez. 1:1; 8:1; 20:1; 24:1, etc.). This use is practically unknown in the writings of the second century.

b. The book of Daniel refers to the months of the calendar by using ordinal numbers (cf. Dan. 10:4) as is the case until the 6th century. It is only after the exile under the Babylonian influence that the months will be indicated by specific names. In Zechariah (1:7), Ezra (6:15; 7:7) and Nehemiah (2:1, 7; 8:1) both systems are still evident.

c. Studies in comparative linguistics have recently revealed that the Aramaic of Daniel features an older structure than the Aramaic of Qumran texts of the 3rd and 2nd century B.C. (cf. T. Murska, "The Aramaic of the Old Targum of Job from Qumran Cave XI," in *Journal of Jewish Studies* 2T [1974]:442; E. Y. Kutscher, "Aramaic," in *Current Trends in Linguistics*, 1970, pp. 400-403; G. L. Archer, "The Aramaic of the 'Genesis Apocryphon' compared with the Aramaic of Daniel," in *New Perspectives on the Old Testament*, 1970, pp. 160-169; cf. G. F. Hasel, "Is the Aramaic of Daniel Early or Late?" *Ministry* [January 1980], pp. 12-13).

d. On the basis of syntactical analysis, evidences have been pointed out that the Aramaic of Daniel denotes an eastern origin and not a western one as would have been expected for a 2nd-century B.C. document (cf. E. Y. Kutscher, "Ha Aramit ha Miqrait Aramit Mizrahit hi o Maaravit?" *First World Congress of Jewish Studies* I, Jerusalem 1952, pp. 123-127).

e. The last but not least argument: the book of Daniel presents itself as a 6th-century writing. If that is indeed the case then the whole thesis of Antiochus Epiphanes is challenged.

[11]See the notes of the Scofield Bible or H. S. Chafer, *Systematic Theology*, Dallas Seminary Press, for a refutation. See H. K. LaRondelle, *The Israel of God in Prophecy*, 1983, pp. 48-52.

[12]See especially G. E. Ladd, *Crucial Questions About the Kingdom of God*, 1952.

[13]For the Jewish sources, see *Miqraoth Gdoloth*, ad loc.; cf. Hersh Goldwurm, *Daniel: A New Translation with a Commentary Anthologized from Talmudic, Midrashic and Rabbinic Sources*, 1979. For the Christian sources cf. L. E. Froom, *The Prophetic Faith of our Fathers*, 1950, vol. 1, see pp. 244ff.

[14]Cf. K. Strand, *Interpreting the Book of Revelation*, 1976, p. 13.

[15]See Desmond Ford, *Daniel*, 1978, p. 69.

[16]Cf. O. Cullmann, *Christ and Time*, 1962, pp. 50ff.

[17]This preoccupation of "close reading" will guide our methodology along the lines we have suggested in Doukhan, *The Genesis Creation Story: Its Literary Structure*, pp. 19ff. For the use of this exegetical method see D. Robertson, "The Bible as Literature," *IDBSup*, p. 550; and especially Meir Weiss, *The Bible from Within*, 1984; cf. the so-called "rhetorical criticism" in, for instance, J. Muilenburg, "Isaiah," *IB* 5:381-418, 422-773.

[18]Our method is similar to that of scholars such as B. S. Childs and J. A. Sanders. For B. S. Childs' methodology see especially his *Introduction to the OT as Scripture*, 1979; J. A. Sanders, *Torah and Canon*, 1979, who lays the foundation of a methodology which sets up the exegesis and the biblical theology against the background of the whole biblical canon.

[19]The *daghesh* in the *Yod* of Daniel is not to obliterate the name of God (cf. C. D. Ginsburg, *Introduction to the Massoretico-Critical Edition of the Hebrew Bible*, 1897, p. 397), but rather to

cut the word in order to emphasize the meaning, playing the function of a disjunctive accent (cf. Israel Yeivin, *Introduction to the Tiberian Massoretes*, 1980, p. 294). This translation of the name of Daniel has also the merit of harmonizing with the grammatical rules which govern the morphology of the names (cf. Fr. Ulmer, *Die Semitischen Eigennamen im Alten Testament*, 1901, pp. 2ff.; cf. J. Doukhan, "Anthroponymie biblique et prophétie," Master's thesis, University of Strasbourg, 1971, p. 12). The importance of judgment in relation to the name of Daniel has been especially pointed out by the apocryphal story of Susanna (see S. B. Hoenig, "Susanna," *IDB* 4:468).

[20]Notice that Ezekiel 14:14, 20 associates Daniel with Noah and Job, within the context of the judgment (cf. vv. 13, 17-22). In the biblical tradition like Daniel (Dan. 3; 6; 12:1, 2, 13), both Noah and Job were indeed the remnant-heroes of God's Judgment: Noah through the flood (cf. Gen. 6-8), and Job through Satan's assaults especially in the setting of the heavenly court in 1:6-12; 2:1-7. Interestingly, the Jerusalem Targum places the first heavenly session on New Year's Day, which is the time of the preliminary judgment, and the second on the Day of Atonement, which is the time of the final judgment (see M.H. Pope, *Job*, 1972, p. 9). See also Job's legal terminology by reference to the heavenly court in 9:15, 32-33; 23:7, etc. and his longing for the resurrection in 19:23-27. In that event, Ezekiel may well have referred to our Daniel (cf. n. 10). The slight spelling difference of the name Daniel (in Ezekiel "Danel," without *yod*) could hardly be an argument against our identification. We know that the *yod* vowel-letter has been added later by the Massoretes (cf. C. D. Ginsburg, pp. 150ff.). On the other hand, the same case is attested, for instance, to Jahzeel in Gen. 46:26, and Jahziel in 1 Chron. 7:13; cf. also the *hey* vowel-letter in Hazael in 2 Kings 8:8 and Hazahel in 2 Kings 8:9; cf. also the marginal note of the *Qere* attached to Ez. 28:3 which refers to our Daniel.

[21]Hartman and Di Lella, p. 208; cf. A. Lacocque, "The veritable centre of the book" (p. 122); cf. Porteous, "The heart of the Book of Daniel" (*Daniel*, 1979, p. 95).

[22]The *goral* (lot, retribution) belongs to the terminology of Judgment (cf. Is. 57:3-6; 17:14). This is especially evident in Daniel 12:13 as it is related to the end of times, conveying the idea of the eschatological retribution. The LXX confirms this idea when it renders "lot" here by glory (*doxa*). Cf. *TDOT* II, pp. 450ff.

[23]Hartman and Di Lella, p. 179.

[24]We may find a parallel with John 8:6 where Jesus writes with His finger on the ground as an act of judgment.

[25]See S. B. Frost, *Old Testament Apocalyptic*, 1952, p. 186; cf. Lacocque, p. 105.

[26]It is therefore not a dittography, see Hartman and Di Lella, p. 183.

[27]See A. Bentzen, *HAT* 1/19 (1952):27-29; cf. Hartman and Di Lella, p. 146.

[28]Hartman and Di Lella, p. 144.

[29]See A. Lacocque, p. 38; cf. J. Pedersen, *Israel: Its Life and Culture*, I, II, 1959, pp. 135-136. This interpretation has already been suggested by LXX and Theodotion who has translated in v. 5 "the word has gone from me."

[30]Cf. the traditional Jewish interpretations; the Targum of Hab. 3:17, Rashi, Ibn Ezra, Metsoudath David, in *Miqraoth Gdoloth*, 1959; cf. Fl. Josephus, *Ant.* X, XI, 7); cf. also the patristic interpretation (Irenaeus, Tertullian, Jerome, Saint Augustine, etc.), in L. E. Froom, *The Prophetic Faith of Our Fathers*, 1950, pp. 244, 245.

[31]Quoted in A. Alba, *Rome et le Moyen Age*, 1964, p. 126.

[32]There is no need to refer to any mythological world to explain Daniel's terminology. The alleged connection with the Babylonian epic of creation, "Enuma Elish," is difficult. The differences

in content and in form are far more striking than what we could see as resemblances. As for the beasts themselves which come out of Tiamat for revenge against Marduk, they have nothing in common with Daniel's beasts. Cf. Hartman and Di Lella, "there is no need here to look for any direct borrowing from ancient mythological literature, such as the Babylonian epic Enuma Elish. Our author could easily have derived his idea . . . from the Bible," p. 212. Cf. M. Delcor, *Le Livre de Daniel*, 1971, p. 145.

[33]"The four winds" designate the four cardinal points (cf. Zech. 2:6; 6:5; Dan. 8:8; 11:4).

[34]Note that the Medes and the Persians are always associated in the book of Daniel wherever the kingdom is referred to (5:28; 6:8, 15; 8:20). This usage clearly indicates the kingdom Daniel is referring to, namely the Medo-Persian empire which is "seen" by Daniel as following Babylon (5:28). The interpretations which disassociate Medes and Persians in order to point to two successive kingdoms is influenced by the concern to make the little horn coincide with Antiochus Epiphanes (cf. among others, A. Lacocque, *The Book of Daniel*, 1979, p. 140).

[35]Cf. Gen. 18:32; Amos 5:3; 6:9; Zech. 8:23; Deut. 23:2; Is. 6:13. Cf. H. A. Brongers, "Die Zehnzahl in der Bibel und ihrer Umwelt," in *Studia Biblica et Semitica: Festschrift Th. C. Vriezen*, 1966, pp. 20-45.

[36]E. R. Thiele proposes the following distribution: Alemani, A.D. 351 (Germany); Franks, A.D. 351 (France); Burgundians, A.D. 406 (Switzerland); Suevi, A.D. 406 (Portugal); Vandals, A.D. 406 (Africa); Visigoths, A.D. 408 (Spain); Saxons, A.D. 449 (Britain); Ostrogoths, A.D. 453 (Italy); Lombards, A.D. 453 (Italy); Heruli, A.D. 476 (Italy)(cf. "Outline Studies in Daniel," mimeographed, 1959). Historians, however differ slightly from each other on the list of these people; cf. Ford, p. 158.

[37]Cf. N. Porteous, *Daniel*, 1979, p. 110.

[38]Cf. Ez. 5:2, 12; Zech. 13:8, 9; Rev. 8:9, 12; 9:18; 12:4; see its usage in Babylonian literature (cf. Theophilus G. Pinches, *An Outline of Assyrian Grammar*, 1910, p. 18).

[39]Note the idiomatic expression "given into his hands" (7:25) which points to the forthcoming oppression (cf. Job 1:12; 2:6).

[40]Literally "times," but in Aramaic, the dual uses the same form as the common plural (cf. F. Rosenthal, *A Grammar of Biblical Aramaic*, 1968, p. 24). The rabbinic tradition reads here "two times" (cf. Ibn Ezra, Rashi etc., in *Miqraoth Gdoloth*, ad loc.).

[41]The Jewish year, which follows the lunar calendar (as does the Babylonian), counts months of 29-30 days. The prophet usually retains the monthly unit of 30 days, which gives a year of 360 days (12x30), making the three years and a half correspond to 1260 days, or 42 months. Cf. Hartman and Di Lella, "Three and a half lunar years would be about 1260 days" (p. 215), with the majority of Jewish and Christian interpreters.

[42]Cf. Porteous, p. 114.

[43]This scene of judgment must include the vision of the death of the animal which is told in vv. 11-12. Daniel relates this event to what he sees in the book, "And the books were opened, I watched then" (vv. 10-11). What the prophet sees is not the execution of the animal but rather the sentence of its death which he reads in the book.

[44]In v. 8, the second interjection is *ʾ^{a}lû* instead of *ʾ^{a}rû* as in the six other instances. Although the two forms are parallel, the *lamed* and the *resh* being phonetically related, we are allowed to think that this break may well reflect the intention of the author to suggest once again the "different" nature of this little horn portrayed with eyes and mouth.

[45]Ibn Ezra's commentary on v. 8:12 in *Miqraoth Gdoloth*; cf. also Rashi and Metsudath David in *Miqraoth Gdoloth*, ad loc.

[46]This methodology which observes "the longitudinal correspondences" on the parallelisms of Hebrew speeches has been especially emphasized by C. Westermann, "Sinn und Grenze religionsgeschichtlicher Parallelen," *Theologische Literaturzeitung* 90 (1965):490-491; cf. also Samuel Sandmel, "Parallelomania," *JBL* 81 (1962):1; cf. J. Doukhan, *The Literary Structure of the Genesis Creation Story*, 1978, pp. 19-30.

[47]This translation better fits the context of dialogue between the two heavenly beings, and is attested to by LXX and Syriac. See Apparatus of *BHS*, ad loc.

[48]Cf. Hartman and Di Lella, p. 226.

[49]Cf. A. Feuillet, who also relates the sanctuary of Daniel 8 to the scene of judgment of Daniel 7 (cf. "Le fils de l'homme de Daniel et la tradition biblique," *Revue Biblique* 60 [1953]:226).

[50]Cf. Hartman and Di Lella, *The Book of Daniel*, p. 147; cf. A. Lacocque, p. 49, cf. p. 102. Cf. Elias Bickerman, *Four Strange Books of the Bible*, 1967, pp. 67-68.

[51]Cf. Jer. 4:7; 49:19; 50:17, 44; Ez. 17:3, 12; Hab. 1:8; cf. O. Zöckler, *The Book of the Prophet Daniel*, 1915, p. 151.

[52]In the Talmud the bear represents the Persian Empire, for the Persians "eat and drink like a bear, are fat like a bear, have long hair like a bear, and are agitated like a bear (*Kidd* 771); cf. *Yoma* 771 which calls the guardian angel of Persia "God's bear."

[53]For the swiftness of the leopard, cf. Hab. 1:8.

[54]Cf. J. E. Hartill, *Biblical Hermeneutics*, 1960, pp. 109-112; cf. Dan. 7:6.

[55]Cf. most commentators who thus justify the thesis of Antiochus Epiphanes; cf. Hartman and Di Lella, "the small horn is pictured as sprouting out of one of the he-goat's four 'conspicuous'

ones, i.e. it represents Epiphanes as a scion of the Seleucid dynasty, one of the four kingdoms that resulted from the breakup of Alexander's kingdom," p. 235; cf. A. Lacocque, *The Book of Daniel*, p. 141; cf. Porteous, *Daniel*, p. 124, etc.

[56]Cf. Hasel, "The 'little horn,' the saints, and the Sanctuary in Daniel 8," in *The Sanctuary and the Atonement*, A. Wallenkampf, W. R. Lesher, eds., 1981, p. 183. Cf. W. Shea, *Selected Studies on Prophetic Interpretation*, p. 42.

[57]Therefore, the phrase does not need to be corrected; cf. *BHS* ad loc.; cf. J. Doukhan, *Aux portes de l'espérance*, pp. 270-272, n. 59.

[58]The word *'ahᵃrîṯ* which has eschatological overtones conveys the idea of a *far* future, the outcome of history and not necessarily of a chronological end (cf. Is. 2:1; Jer. 48:47; 49:39; Ez. 38:8; cf. especially Dan. 10:14; cf. T. Boman, *Hebrew Thought Compared with Greek*, 1960, p. 149; cf. H. Seebass, "*acharith*," *Theological Dictionary of the Old Testament*, J. Botterweck, H. Ringgren, eds., 1977, pp. 207-212). Obviously, in our context it relates to all the kingdoms and not only to the immediately preceding four. This word is used in two parallel expressions before and after the whole series of kingdoms is mentioned so as to frame them:

-v. 19	*be'ahᵃrîṯ hazzā'am* (far after the indignation)
-vv. 20-22	All the kingdoms
-v. 23	*be'ahᵃrîṯ malḵûtām* (far after these kingdoms)

The similarity between v. 19 and v. 23 shows that since the expression of v. 19 embraces the whole series of kingdoms, it must be the same for v. 23. "*be'ahᵃrîṯ*" points to the same far horizon in both verses. For this literary device see the introduction and the conclusion in the Genesis Creation story (Genesis 1:1 and 2:4a), cf. Peter Weimar, "Die Toledot-Formel in der priesterschriftlichen Geschichtsdarstellung," *BZ* 18 (1974):73-74. Cf. J. Doukhan, *The Genesis Creation Story*, p. 206, n.2 and pp. 251-252.

[59]*Hebrew and Aramaic Dictionary of the Old Testament,* p. 232; cf. L. Koehler and W. Baumgartner, *Lexicon in Veteris Testamenti Libros*, p. 794.

[60]See his commentary in *Miqraoth Gdoloth*, ad loc.

[61]*Jewish Encyclopedia*, "Atonement," vol. 2, p. 286.

[62]Cf. A. Lacocque, pp. 172-173; cf. W. Porteous, *Daniel*, 1979, p. 130.

[63]See J. Doukhan, "The Seventy Weeks of Daniel 9: An Exegetical Study," *AUSS* 17(1979):4-5.

[64]Ibid. pp. 19-22.

[65]This is its only use in the Bible; *neḥtak* is an *hapax legomenon.* Our translation is supported by related semitic languages. See W. von Soden, *Akkadisches Handwörterbuch*, 1965, v. 5 *ḥtk.* Moreover this meaning is attested to in the Mishnah in most cases (28 instances with the sense of cutting against only 3 with the sense of determining). See M. Jastrow, *A Dictionary of the Targumim, The Talmud Babli and Yerushalmi, and the Midrashic Literature*, 1963, s.v. *ḥtk.*

[66]Probably the same concern governs the change of languages within the book of Daniel. When the text concerns the Israelite economy it is written in Hebrew (ch. 1-2:4a; 8-12); when it concerns the nations, it is written in Aramaic (ch. 2:4b to ch. 7:28). Cf. Otto Plöger, *Das Buch Daniel*, 1965, p. 26. Instead of being an argument on behalf of the division of the book, the changing of languages would plead on behalf of its profound unity. Cf. H. H. Rowley, "The Unity of the Book of Daniel," *Hebrew Union College Annual* 23 (1950-51):223-273.

[67]Cf. J. Doukhan, *Drinking at the Sources*, p, 134, p. 178.

[68]Cf. Hartman and Di Lella, p. 278; cf. E. S. Horton, *Daniel*, 1973, p. 52.

[69]Cf. T. B. *Marzin* 326, *Yoma* 54a; *Midrash Rabbah, Eikah* Pq. 34, etc.

[70]Cf. W. Shea, *Selected Studies on Prophetic Interpretation*, 1982, pp. 89-93.

[71]For a detailed exposition of the historical fulfillment of the prophecy and the date of 457 for the decree of Ezra, see S. H. Horn and L. H. Wood, *The Chronology of Ezra 7*, 1953, pp. 91-92; cf. L. Wood, *A Commentary on Daniel*, 1976, pp. 251-254.

[72]Cf. especially the form *nišlaḥ* (to be forgiven) in Lev. 4:20, 26, 31, 35; 5:16 etc., in parallel with *kpr*. Cf. also other verbs in Lev. 7:20, 21, 27; cf. 19:7. Cf. G. J. Wenham, *The Book of Leviticus*, 1979, pp. 125, 241. Cf. H. K. LaRondelle, *Perfection and Perfectionism*, 1975, p. 127. Cf. R. M. Hals, *Grace and Faith in the Old Testament*, 1980, p. 43. Cf. G. von Rad, "The Beginnings of Historical Writings in Ancient Israel," in *The Problem of the Hexateuch and Other Essays*, 1966, pp. 201-204.

[73]Cf. *Sir* 45:24 where the word *prostates*: prince designates the High Priest; cf. Fl. Josephus, *Ant.* XII, r, 2; cf. 1 Macc. 13:42.

[74]The personage is not Gabriel as some commentators have argued (cf. A. Bentzen, N. Porteous, H. L. Ginsberg, etc.). As R. H. Charles and A. Lacocque point out, Daniel is not affected by the apparition of Gabriel (Dan. 9:21; 10:16) whereas he is affected by the vision of this personage and needs to be strengthened three times (10:8, 9, 10, 15, 18, 19). Cf. J. A. Montgomery, *A Critical and Exegetical Commentary on the Book of Daniel*, 1950, p. 420, and A. Lacocque, *The Book of Daniel*, p. 206. Note the same description of the Son of Man in Rev. 1:13-15 and 2:18; cf. Ez. 9:2, 3, 11. Moreover the Septuagint translates the word "clothed in linen" in Dan. 12:6, 7 as in the texts of Ezekiel with the same Greek word *bussina*, the technical term for the priestly cloth. The

personage is then described in the same terms as the divine Majesty in Ezekiel and must be identified as Michael (cf. A. Lacocque, *Daniel*, p. 206). Significantly the Jewish tradition, probably inspired by these texts, has described Michael as the Heavenly High Priest (see Hag. 12b; cf. *The Jewish Encyclopedia*, vol. 10, p. 625).

[75]The same language is used further in this passage (Heb. 9:27, 28) where human death and the judgment are in parallelism with Christ's death and His second coming. Death, Judgment, the cross and the Parousia are associated not because they belong to the same time, but rather because they stand in the same eschatological perspective. We may also note the trend of this epistle to synchronize events which are yet distant in time. In the same way the connection between the Day of Atonement and the Cross does not imply that the two events belong to the same time. The argument of the epistle lies on a theological level, focusing on the "better" value of Christ's blood rather than on a historical or chronological level to localize the time of the event of the Cross in regard to the Day of Atonement (see W. G. Johnsson, *Defilement and Purgation in the Book of Hebrews*, 1973, ch. 4).

[76]Cf. C. L. Milton, "Atonement," *IDB* 1:310. Cf. Koehler-Baumgartner, *Lexicon*, pp. 451, 452.

[77]Cf. Y. Kaufmann, *The Religion of Israel*, 1960, p. 114; cf. G. Hasel, "Studies in Biblical Atonement II: The Day of Atonement," in *The Sanctuary and the Atonement*, A.V. Wallenkampf, W. R. Lesher, eds., 1981, pp. 122, 123.

[78]See Gesenius, Kautzsch, Cowley, *Hebrew Grammar*, 1910, pp. 313ff.; G. H. A. von Ewald, *Syntax of the Hebrew Language*, 1870, p. 7; J. Doukhan, "L'Hébreu en Vie," 1973, pp. 103-104.

[79]See Gesenius, Kautzsch, Cowley, pp. 309ff., and especially William Turner, "The Tenses of the Hebrew Verb," in *Studies Biblical and Oriental*, 1876, pp. 338-407.

[80]Cf. Deut. 16:20, Is. 42:21, Prov. 8:20, Is. 56:1, etc. Cf. Koehler-Baumgartner, *Lexicon*, pp. 794-795.

[81]This "time" dimension of wisdom is one of the prevailing ideas in wisdom literature (cf. Eccl. 3; 8:5; cf. Prov. 25:13, 19; Job 14:14; cf. also the text of Eph. 5:15-16 which stands in the same line relating wisdom and time).

[82]Cf. Lacocque, p. 234; Is. 26:17ff.; Matt. 24:21.

[83]This Psalm, which is concerned with God's forgiveness, ends with the specific technical expression attached to the Day of Atonement, "all his iniquities;" cf. Lev. 16:21, 22.

[84]This Psalm belongs to the Jewish liturgy of the Day of Atonement. See "The Prayers of Rosh Hashana," in *Shulkhan Aruch*, ch. CIC, 582.

[85]See M. Delcor, *Le Livre de Daniel*, 1971, p. 259. See W. Zimmerli, *Man and His Hope in the Old Testament*, 1968, p. 46.

[86]This link with the core of the book of Daniel testifies to the unity of the book and does not allow the commonly admitted theory of glosses for this passage (Hartman and Di Lella, p. 313).

[87]This blessing includes those of 1844 as well as those coming after 1844. To say "Blessed are those who come to 1844" amounts to saying "Blessed are those who reach the period which starts in 1844." If we translate this language in spacial terms, "blessed are those who reach point A" would of course include those who have gone beyond point A and may now be in B. Let us not forget that 1844 indicates the *point of termination* of a period and not the date of a definite event.

[88]See Dan. 9:27 where the same expression applies to the Romans; cf. the interpretation of Jesus in Matt. 24:15; cf. Mark 13:14. Cf. D. Ford, *Daniel*, p. 63.

[89]Against C. Schedl, "Mystische Arithmetik oder geschichtliche Zahlen (Dan. 8:14; 12:11-13)," *BZ* 8 (1964):101-105.

[90]W. Ullmann, *A Short History of the Papacy in the Middle Ages*, 1972, p. 37. H. M. Gwatwim, J. P. Whitney, ed., *The Cambridge Medieval History*, 1936, p. 285-286; cf. S. Pointer, *A History of the Middle Ages*, 1965, p. 28-29.

[91]Thus Gregory the Great (590-604) is the first who exercises the prerogatives of both church and state. W. Ullmann, *Principles of Government and Politics in the Middle Ages*, 1961, pp. 60-61.

[92]See Y. Congar, *L'Eglise de St. Augustin à l'époque moderne*, 1970, p. 32; cf. W. Ullmann, pp. 60ff.

[93]See W. F. Church, *The Influence of the Enlightenment on the French Revolution*, 1974.

[94]The book of Revelation refers to the same event in terms of a "deadly wound" (Rev. 13:3, 12) which will be healed. History shows indeed that the papal power has been restored as early as the 19th century in the wake of Catholic revival (George L. Mosse, *The Culture of Western Europe*, 1961, p. 35-38).

[95]See P. Prigent, *L'Apocalypse de Saint Jean*, 1981, p. 9; Albrecht Oepke, "αποκαλυπτϖ," in *Theologisches Wörterbuch zum Neuen Testament*, ed. by G. Kittel and G. Friedrich, 3:586ff.

[96]See U. B. Müller, *Messias und Menschensohn in Jüdischen Apokalypsen und in der Offenbarung des Johannes*, 1972; cf. P. Prigent, p. 27.

[97]The Greek word *poderes* for robe is found nowhere else in the New Testament but is used in the LXX for the specific garment of the High Priest (in LXX see Ex. 25:6, 7; 28:4; Ez. 9:2, 3, 11; etc.). Cf. Fl. Josephus, *Ant.* III, 153ff.; Iraneus, *Adv. Haer.* 4, 20; cf. most commentators; especially O. Cullmann, *The Christology of the New Testament*, 1959, pp. 104-105; Prigent, p. 28.

[98]That this vision of the day of Judgment is given on the "day of the Lord" may lend the meaning of the latter expression in the sense of the Sabbath (see K. A. Strand, "Another Look at 'Lord's Day' in the Early Church and in Rev 1:10," *NTS* 13 [1966-67]:174-81). This association, which points out the eschatological dimension of the Sabbath is suggested in the OT (Ezek. 46:1, 3, 10-12; Is. 66:22, 23) and is particularly vivid in Jewish Tradition (T.B. *Sanhedrin* 98a; cf. Theodore Friedman, "The Sabbath: Anticipation of Redemption," *Judaism* 16 [1967]:144ff.), as well as in the New Testament (see Heb. 4:3-6, 11-15). Indeed, the association of the Sabbath and *the* day of the Lord was theologically justified because the Sabbath was referred to in biblical tradition, in a genitive connection to the Lord, it was the Sabbath of the Lord (Ex. 31:13; 16:23; 20:10; Lev. 23:3; cf. also the statement "the Son of Man is the Lord of the Sabbath," Mat. 12:8, which is "a covert reference to the Lord's day" [W. Stott, "A Note on the Word KYRIAKH in Rev 1:10," *NTS* 12 (1965-66):70-75]). On the other hand, the reference to the "Lord's day" does not necessarily mean that John was transported to the future glorious day of the Lord (S. Bacchiocchi, *From Sabbath to Sunday*, 1977, p. 124), an interpretation which does not do justice to the context and the Greek syntax of the passage (F. Düsterdieck, *Critical and Exegetical Handbook to the Revelation of John*, 1887, p. 109). Moreover, this association on the level of the existence of the prophet is already used in the OT; see for instance Daniel and Ezekiel, who have their vision of the Day of Atonement while they are celebrating this feast in their actual time (Dan. 10:1, Ezek. 40:1). It is also noteworthy that this way of connecting the active day of Feast and the messianic event taking place then is familiar to the language of John in his Gospel (see Leon Morris, *The Gospel According to John*, 1971, pp. 342, 394, 436). This typology of the Sabbath may well have inspired Jesus as he chose to perform his miracles on that very day (see Bacchiocchi, p. 19ff.; cf. J. Danielou, *Bible and Liturgy*, 1956, p. 226). This observation may well confirm the intuition of some scholars who, "given the many liturgical allusions in Revelation" have surmised that "John may have had this vision during the liturgical service" (J. Massyngberde Ford, *Revelation*, 1975, p. 382).

[99]See K. Strand, *Interpreting the Book of Revelation*, 1976, pp. 51-52.

[100]See E. Lohmeyer, "Die Offenbarung des Johannes," *Handbuch zum Neuen Testament*, 1953, p. 119.

[101]Note the function of the number four which marks the progression of human history as in the book of Daniel (cf. n. 50). It is also noteworthy that if we consider A as being the Introduction (no action there), and I, the conclusion, we remark that the text is divided into 7 sections (B-H), an important number in the apocalyptic language. The two structures (4 steps and 7 sections) do not repudiate each other but support each other instead.

[102]That section G (Rev. 14:1-5) is indeed concerned with the Judgment is indicated by the common motifs shared by this passage and Rev. 11:16-19 which deals specifically with the Judgment (note especially v.18). The motifs are: loud voices and thunder (Rev. 14:2; cf. 11:15, 19); heavenly thrones (14:3; cf. 11:16); the elders (14:3; cf. 11:16); and the act of judgment (14:5; cf. 11:18).

[103]The other beast with two horns like a lamb (vv. 11-18) plays only a secondary role in our passage, essentially supporting and promoting the ten-horned beast (cf. 13:12, 15). "Its only *raison d'être* is to promote the worship of the Beast with 10 horns of which it is the servant" (P. Prigent, p. 209).

[104]Cf. P. Prigent, p. 200.

[105]In both passages the expression "son of man" is used with the same indefinite form and not like the traditional formula of the gospels, "the son of the man" (cf. Matt. 16:27; 24:27; Mark 13:26; Luke 18:8; John 3:13; etc.). The text of Dan. 7 seems therefore to be more than any other text in the mind of the author of Rev. 14; see J. Coppens, "La mention d'un Fils de l'homme angélique en Ap. 14:14," in J. Lambrecht, *L'Apocalypse johannique et l'Apocalyptique dans le Nouveau Testament*, 1980, p. 229.

[106]The intervention of God after the flood is mentioned here in terms of Creation. The structure of this passage (Gen. 8-9) eloquently reflects the first Genesis Creation story (Gen. 1:1-2:4a). The similarities between our two texts are striking, following the same division in 7 sections:

1. The wind over the earth and waters. Gen. 8:1; cf. Gen.1:2.
2. Division of waters. Gen. 8:2-5; cf. Gen. 1:6-8.
3. Appearance of plants. Gen. 8:6-12; cf. Gen. 1:9-13.
4. Appearance of light. Gen. 8:13-14; cf. Gen. 1:14-19.
5. Deliverance of animals. Gen. 8:15-17; cf. Gen. 1:20-23.
6. Animals together with men, blessing, food for men, image of God. Gen. 8:18-9:7; cf. Gen. 1:24-31.
7. Sign of covenant. Gen. 9:8-17; cf. Gen. 2:1-3.

For the connection between Creation and the Flood, see Ps. 74:12-17, cf. 2 Pet. 3:5-13. See also W. A. Gage, *The Gospel of Genesis,* 1984, pp. 16-20.

[107]Here again we find the same reference to Creation. Abraham is called to "get out" of darkness with the same rhythm in 7 words ("I will show," "I will make," "I will bless you," "I will make your name great," "I will bless," "I will curse in you all the families"). Note that the first six words are all molded in the same pattern (imperfect, first person); the seventh word is different and conveys the result of the six preceding actions (cf. Gen. 2:1-3; for the difference of the seventh action in regard to the previous six, see Doukhan, *The Genesis Creation Story*, pp. 41-43).

[108]The event of Exodus has traditionally been referred to as a new Creation (Ex. 15:8; Deut 4:32-33; Is. 43:1-3). For the connection between the building of the tabernacle and the Creation story of Gen. 1, see Peter J. Kearnay, "The P Redaction of Exodus 25-40," *ZAW* 89 (1977):375-387.

[109]See especially Deut. 34:6. The absence of any tomb witnessing to Moses' death, which has been perceived as a mystery ("no one knows . . ."), is a hint of his resurrection; cf. Jude 9. Cf. Mark 9:4; cf. the Jewish pseudepigraph, the *Assumption of Moses*, and in rabbinic literature, *Dukkah* 5a.

[110]The book of Leviticus begins in connection with the last verse of Exodus (Ex. 40:38: "The cloud of the Lord was above the Tabernacle;" cf. Lev. 1:1, "the Lord called to Moses from the tabernacle"). Likewise, the book of Leviticus ends in connection with the beginning of Numbers (Lev. 27:34: "The Lord spoke to Moses on Mount Sinai;" cf. Num. 1:1, "The Lord spoke to Moses in the Wilderness of Sinai"). This linkage to the preceding and the following books situates the book of Leviticus in the middle of the Pentateuch. Cf. G. T. Wenham, *The Book of Leviticus*, 1979, p. 6.

[111]The book of Leviticus is set within a narrative framework "and YHWH spoke to Moses saying" which occurs 36 times. The 18th occurrence, i.e. in the middle of the 36, introduces Lev. 16 which deals with the Day of Atonement, and marks also the theological center of the book. Note Keil and Delitzsch: "Whilst, therefore, the laws of sacrifice and purification on the one hand, culminate in the institution of the *yearly day of atonement*, so on the other do those relating to the sanctification of life culminate in the appointment of the *Sabbatical and jubilee years*; and thus the two series of laws in Leviticus are placed in unmistakeable correspondence to one another" (*The Pentateuch* II, n.d., pp. 263-264). Cf. Dan. 7 and Rev. 14 which also lie at the very center of their books.

[112]*Shulkhan Aruch*, ch. CCXV, II.

[113]The phrase "evenings and mornings" has then nothing to do with a late post-exilic language (cf. R. de Vaux, *Ancient Israel: Its Life and Institutions*, 1961, p. 181). On the other hand, the bridge between Gen. 1 and Dan. 8:14 does not allow the view which interprets "evenings and mornings" in the sense of half a day, on the basis of the two sacrifices of evening and morning (for the equation 2300 evenings and mornings as amounting to 1150 days, see esp. A. Lacocque, pp. 249-250). It is also noteworthy that this phrase does not belong to the cultic language since the latter uses rather the morning-evening sequence; see J. B. Segal, "Intercalation and the Hebrew Calendar," in *VT* 7 (1957):254.

[114]This is indicated by the numerous references to atonement and forgiveness (vv. 3, 9, 10, 12, 17) and especially through the specific expression traditionally attached to this festival: "all the iniquities" (v. 3; cf. Lev. 16:21).

[115]See *Mishna Arachin* II, 6. Cf. 6 *Shab* 118b.

[116]See *Entsiklopedia Miqraith* 3:595, 1965. Cf. K. Hrubi, "Le Yom ha-Kippurim ou Jour de l'Expiation," *Old Testament Studies* 10 (1965):58ff. Cf. the Beney Israel in India who celebrate both festivals in the same unit (J. Van Goudoever, *Fêtes et Calendriers bibliques*, 1967, pp. 57ff.).

[117]See K. G. Kuhn, "Babylon," in *Theological Dictionary of the New Testament*, I, 1964, pp. 514-517.

[118]Cf. G. von Rad, *Theology of the Old Testament*, p. 193.

[119]The word is *hatamîd* (which means "the continual"), implying what the Bible specifies as "the continual offering." This expression occurs 103 times in its complete form (cf. Koehler-Baumgartner, *Lexicon*, p. 103). The abbreviated form has been used in Daniel under the influence of the concise style of the prophetic oracle. Incidentally, the same abbreviated form *hatamîd* has been used in Talmudic literature (see M. Jastrow, *Dictionary of the Targumim*, 1963, pp. 1676-1677).

[120]This typical expression applies in the Bible to the fall of a city like Babylon (Is. 21:9; cf. Rev. 18:2) or Jerusalem (Lam. 1:9) or even to the fall of Satan (Luke 10:18).

[121]This connection between the act of atonement in the Most Holy and the Ten Commandments may be supported on the linguistic level as far as the word *deḇîr* (the back of the sanctuary) is etymologically related to the word *deḇarîm* (commandments); cf. F. Torrance, *Royal Priesthood*, 1955, pp. 1ff.

[122]For the importance of this language hence the necessity for exegesis to take this fact in consideration see A. Berkeley Mickelsen, *Interpreting the Bible*, 1963, pp. 185-186.

[123]The Bible associates the divine control of time with the Creation (Jer. 31:35-36) and the concept of eternity (everlasting time) with the Sabbath (Is. 66:22-24); on the importance of the time element in Sabbath, see esp. A. Heschel, *The Sabbath: Its Meaning for Modern Man*, 1976, p. 10.

[124]The very phrase of Dan. 7:25, "changes times and law," belongs to the Sabbath evening prayers.

[125]Cf. S. Bacchiocchi, *From Sabbath to Sunday: A Historical Investigation of the Rise of Sunday Observance in Early Christianity*, 1977; cf. J. Doukhan, *Drinking at the Sources*, 1981, pp. 23-27. The movement was gradual; it first started timidly at the end of the first century (see the isolated remarks of Ignatius in his Epistle to the Magnesians, ch. 8:1, 2) then in the Marcionite heresy (2nd century). The decisive input is finally given by the imperial and church councils of the 4th century. The concern of this movement is in no way religious; it manifests the beginnings of anti-Jewish hatred and the desire to compromise with the pagan religion, as clearly evidenced in the decrees:

> The Emperor Constantine to A. Helpidius.
> All Judges, townspeople and all occupations should rest on the most honorable day of the sun.
> (Code of Justinian III, 12 *de feriis*, 3)

> Christians must not judaize by resting on the Sabbath, but must work on that day . . . however, if any shall be found judaizing, let them be anathema from Christ.
> (Canon 29 of the Council of Laodicea)

[126]The reminiscences of Ex. 31:12, especially on the common motif of "sanctify" (cf. also Gen. 2:1-3) indicate that Ezekiel is

dealing with the same Sabbath, i.e. the 7th day of the week, the memorial of Creation.

[127]Lacocque, p. 21; see also Hartman and Di Lella, p. 129.

[128]See Hartman and Di Lella, p. 133; Wood, *A Commentary on Daniel*, 1976, p. 37.

[129]They were given new names in the overall desire to make them subject to the new gods, inasmuch as their names were Babylonian names of God; see Lacocque, pp. 29-30.

[130]Lacocque, pp. 86-87.

[131]Charles L. Feinberg, *The Prophecy of Ezekiel*, 1969, p. 161-163.

[132]See J. Doukhan, "The Seventy Weeks," p. 16.

[133]The interpretation of "the first month" (10:4) as referring to Tishri rather than to Nisan (the general interpretation) would be supported by a number of indications:

1. Both Dan. 10 and Ezek. 40 deal with the same vision of the heavenly High Priest. In Ezek. 40, the content of the Vision which brings up the High Priest dressed for the Day of Atonement, is associated with the date of the vision. It takes place at the beginning of the year on the 10th day of the month, which allows us to think that the vision is actually given at the Day of Atonement, as it has been defended in Jewish Tradition (see *Miqraoth Gdoloth*, ad loc). Therefore, since both texts deal with the same material, the vision of the heavenly High Priest, and since they are both dated at the beginning of the year, we can interpret this time in Dan. 10 as also referring to the Day of Atonement.

2. Dan. 10 (v. 4) also points to 2 Chron. 7:10 which deals with the dedication of the Temple; both refer to the same period of time, 23 days, and in both texts the 24th day is the day when God's vision is given as an answer to man's prayer (see the common unity between the two texts on the hearing of the prayer, 2 Chron.

7:12; cf. Dan. 10:12). In 2 Chron. 7 the event is dated at the 7th month which in this context points to Tishri (see esp. v. 9 which undoubtedly points to the Feast of Tabernacles of Lev. 23:39); the parallels between the two texts may indicate that Dan. 10 also refers to Tishri though following a different calendar (see Ed. R. Thiele, *A Chronology of the Hebrew Kings*, 1977, p. 14ff.).

3. Actually the Tishri interpretation would better fit the context of Dan. 10 which tells us about fasting and conveying a hint to the Day of Atonement (see A. Lacocque, p. 205) than the Nisan interpretation. The latter would put Daniel in the context of Passover (see here Ibn Ezra's argument against the Nisan interpretation on the basis that Daniel would have then transgressed the commandments regulating the observance of Passover, in *Miqraoth Gdoloth*, ad loc). Moreover, the Tishri celebrations, in which the Day of Atonement (the 10th) takes the central place also fit the precision of the giving of the vision on the 24th of this month (10:4). The latter falls then exactly at the end of the whole cycle of festivals, hence immediately following the feast of Tabernacles (Lev. 23:39), i.e., the feast which remembers the hope for the promised land (Lev. 23:43; cf. A. P. Bloch, *The Biblical and Historical Background of Jewish Customs and Ceremonies*, 1980, p. 182), and typologically points to the eschatological hope of the kingdom of God (cf. Zech. 14:16ff.; Is. 2:2-4; 56:6-8; cf. Robert Martin-Archard, *Essai biblique sur les fêtes d'Israel*, 1979, pp. 87, 92).

Besides the rich meaning this reference may convey, the association with the Tigris in this context may also be intended to remind us of Cyrus' attacks against the Babylonian army which took place as well on the Tigris and in Tishri (see W.H. Shea, "The Location and Significance of Armageddon in Rev 16:16," *AUSS* 18 [1980]:157). This episode is still fresh in Daniel's memory, since the message is revealed "in the third year of Cyrus" (Dan. 10:1). The battle implied in Dan. 10-11 would then have the same historical setting as the battle of Armageddon in Rev. 16 (see W.H. Shea, ibid., pp. 157-162).

[134]The first word "And I" (11:1 in the Hebrew text) links to the preceding verse, the last one of chapter 10. See also the strong common wording between the introduction of chapter 11 and the conclusion of chapter 10. "It is generally agreed that

these chapters belong together as a single whole" (N.W. Porteous, *Daniel*, 1965, p. 149).

[135]"List of the Persian (Achaemenid) emperors:

Cyrus 550-529
Cambyses 529-521
Darius I 521-485
Xerxes I 485-465
Artaxerxes I 465-424
Xerxes II 424-423
Darius II 423-404
Artaxerxes II 404-359
Artaxerxes III 359-338
Arses 338-336
Darius III 336-330"

(Philip K. Hitti, *The Near East in History: A 5000 Year Story*, 1961, p. 55).

[136]As for the so-called false Smerdis (521) who is included in the list of some commentators (see E. Bickermann, *Four Strange Books*, p. 117ff.; Desmond Ford, *Daniel*, p. 260) it is omitted here because he ruled less than one year (actually 7 months) and was an imposter of a median origin (see L. Wood, *A Commentary on Daniel*, 1976, p. 281). The prophecy specifies a Persian origin (Dan. 11:2). On the other hand, the ommission may also be grounded on the simple fact that this reign may well have been forged by Darius himself who spread the news of a "false Smerdis" to justify his ascension to the throne; this official story was then accepted and passed on by Herodotus. As the historian Isaac Asimov recognizes: "It may be one of those cases where a great lie has been foisted on history" (*The Near East: 10,000 Years of History*, 1968, p. 125). As a matter of fact, Smerdis is ignored in the list of most commentators (See Hartman and DiLella, p. 288).

[137]This view is adopted in Jewish tradition by Ibn Ezra, Ralbag, Ibn Yachiah and Malbim; see Rabbis Nesson, Sherman, Meir, Zlotowitz, *Daniel*, 1979, p. 283; see also *Rosh Hashanah* 2b. There is actually no consensus among biblical scholars as to who these

four kings are. See Hartman and Di Lella, p. 288; cf. Delcor, pp. 218-219. For a survey of the opinions of the older commentaries, see O. Plöger, *Das Buch Daniel*, pp. 157-158; Lacocque, pp. 160-161.

[138]A. Bonifacio, P. Maréchal, *Histoire: Orient-Grèce*, 1963, pp. 99, 199; cf. J. Bright, *A History of Israel*, p. 374. Cf. Diodore XI, 71, 74, 77.

[139]Isaac Asimov, *The Near East: 10,000 Years of History*, p. 136; cf. also Herodotus VI, p. 106.

[140]For Artexerxes' wealth see George Rawlinson, *The Five Great Monarchies of the Ancient World*, 1887, I, p. 31, 32; III, p. 478, 480. Cf. Herodotus I, 192.

[141]Cf. O. Plöger, *Das Buch Daniel*, KAT, 18, 1965, ad loc.; A. Lacocque, p. 159. Other common wordings are noted between Dan. 9 and 11 especially on the motif of conflict: *nāḡîd* (prince) in Dan. 9:25; cf. Dan. 11:22; *šṭp* (inundation) in Dan. 9:26 and Dan. 11:10, 22, 26, 40, and especially *šmm* (desolation) in Dan. 9:26, 27 and Dan. 11:31. Cf. Doukhan, "The Seventy Weeks of Daniel 9," p. 16; cf. W. H. Shea, *Selected Studies*, p. 47-48.

[142]Cf. Hartman and Di Lella, p. 287.

[143]Hartman and Di Lella, p. 288.

[144]Cf. Lacocque, p. 161.

[145]See S. R. Driver, *Daniel*, p. 164; Lacocque, p. 217; Delcor, p. 220. Cf. also Rashi and Ibn Ezra in *Miqraoth Gdoloth*, ad loc.

[146]The only other biblical passage where *'ahᵃrîṯ* could be understood in the sense of posterity is found in Ps 109:13. But here also the context implies rather a temporal sequence since this word parallels the expression "the generation following" (cf. W. Rudolf, KAT, XIII/2 contra H. Seebass, in *Theological Dictionary of the Old Testament*, Botterweck and Ringgren, eds., vol. I, p. 211).

[147]This period in Daniel's vision includes the time of the division into kingdoms. The 10 horns are indeed integrated into the fourth kingdom (cf. 7:24a and p. 24).

[148]This interpretation is to our knowledge not advocated elsewhere. I must recognize that I stand quite alone here. Most interpreters would perceive in this passage clear references to the war between Seleucids (the King of the North) and Ptolemies (the King of the South), taking us up to the reign of Antiochus Epiphanes to which the most important section (vv. 21-45) is directed (see N.W. Porteous, *Daniel*, pp. 156-157). Even among conservative scholars one would hold the view that at least vv. 5-13 contain allusions to the Seleucids-Ptolemies conflict. The second section (vv. 14-30) would either deal with Rome or with Antiochus Epiphanes and the third section (31-34) would deal with the little horn. The last section (vv. 40-46) would deal with the time of the end with references either to Turkey or the Papacy as being the King of the North (See SDA BC IV:868-869, 876; cf. W. H. Shea, *Selected Studies on Prophetic Interpretation*, pp. 44-55). It seems to us that these interpretations stumble on two main difficulties. (1) In addition to the linguistic links between Dan. 11:22, 31, 32-34 respectively to ch. 9, 8 or 7, we have other links within chapter 11 itself (see the literary structure of Daniel 11). Thus if the chronology of chapter 11 is established on the basis of its binding to chapters 7, 8, 9, then it also has to take into account the internal links between verses of chapter 11 itself. As an example, if I say 11:22 points to 9:24-27, therefore referring to the same event, I must also say that since I find links between two sections of chapter 11, I am allowed to think that they are dealing with the same event. (2) The reference North-South goes beyond 11:13 up to the end of the chapter implying a lack of consistency in this interpretation. If we recognize that the king of the North is the little horn in v. 31, for example, we must think the same when it is referred to before and after v. 31. Furthermore, if we interpret the conflict North-South in a spiritual manner from v. 40 on we must be consistent and apply the same reading elsewhere in the chapter (see G. McGready Price, *The*

Greatest of the Prophets, 1955, p. 314 and his book *The Time of the End*, 1967; cf. D. Ford, p. 274ff.; cf. F. W. Hardy, p. 223).

[149]This literary observation does not contradict the one we made in regard to the chiastic structure relating chapters 7 and 12. We are not dealing here with the structure of the passage *per se*, but with the connections between passages which may work on the basis of different emphases and perspectives. See for instance the parallelisms in the book of Zechariah where ABCD of 8:22-10:3a not only parallels ABCD of 1-2:9 but is also in chiastic structure with the next material C_1B_1 (Strand, p. 83, 85).

[150]The identification of the little horn coming after Rome with the power of the North makes then the thesis of Antiochus Epiphanes in Daniel 11 difficult to be defended.

[151]This rhythm in seven steps suggests already the symbolic significance of the process which is described here; number seven "represents a mystic cycle . . . within which God accomplishes His purposes" (L. A. Muirhead, "Numbers," *Dictionary of the Apostolic Church*, ed. by James Hastings, New York, 1918, p. 92). Indeed several evidences show the importance of this number in our context: the ritual arrangements in the Pentateuch (see for instance the Sabbatical year, the Jubilee, etc.), the frequent symbolic use of this number in apocalyptic literature, and especially the role number seven plays in the book of Daniel (see chapter 9). In fact, in the Bible as well as in contemporary extrabiblical literature "this is the only number which appears to be used symbolically with any consistency" (John J. Davis, *Biblical Numerology*, Ann Arbor, Mich., 1968, p. 116; cf. M. H. Pope, "Number, Numbering, Numbers," *IDB* 3:561-566). It is also noteworthy that this rhythm of seven has often been used in the Bible to mold the literary structure (for instance the Creation story in Gen. 1-2, and also the story of the building of the Sanctuary in Ex. 25-40; see respectively Jacques B. Doukhan, *The Genesis Creation Story*, pp. 39-52, and Peter J. Kearney, pp. 375-87).

[152]The literary structure has recently been studied by F. N. Hardy, "An Historicist Perspective in Daniel 11," Master's Thesis, Andrews University, 1983. Although this author recognizes some connections between these passages (see esp. pp. 113-120), he fails to perceive the longitudinal parallelism. He draws a huge chiasm from ch. 10 to 12 which is in some instances convincing and interesting yet is weak in some others where the linguistic support is not provided (see for instance the correspondence established between 11:2 and 11:40 on the vague connection between "stir up" and "engage," p. 112).

[153]Notice here also this rhythm in four, which is familiar to the language of Daniel, marking the limits of the earthly kingdoms (cf. notes 50 and 101).

[154]Cf. Strand's two cautions in regard to the hermeneutic of literary analysis in the book of Revelation. "First, care must be taken to avoid any methodology which would make the messages of Revelation either entirely historical or entirely eschatological, for such would do violence to the book's division into major historical and eschatological parts. Second, it would likewise be inappropriate to adopt a system of interpretation which would claim that the messages of the Apocalypse portrayed an absolutely 'straight-line' or completely sequential chain of events or developments" (*Interpreting the Book of Revelation*, 1976, p. 53).

[155]See especially the connection on the same Hebrew words *ḥzq* (strengthen in 11:1 and uphold in 10:21) and *'emet̲* (truth in 11:2 and 10:21); cf. A. Lacocque p. 216; cf. note 140.

[156]See R. A. Bowman, "The North Country," *IDB* 3:560.

[157]See Clifford, *Cosmic Mountain*, 1972, p. 3. Cf. M. H. Pope, *'El' in the Ugaritic Texts*, 1955, pp. 95, 86, 100, 102.

[158]Cf. A. Keil and F. Delitzsch, *Commentary on the Old Testament,* 1982, 9B, p. 433; cf. Dan. 11:43.

[159]See J. P. Lange, *The Revelation of John: A Commentary on the Holy Scriptures*, vol. X, 1874, p. 225; cf. D. Ford, pp. 276-277.

[160]This passage is either interpreted as an "Imaginative Prediction of Antiochus' death" (Hartman and DiLella, p. 303; cf. Delcor, p. 247) or a prediction of a future Antichrist (Keil, p. 461-467). For all the commentators the text should not be taken literally (Lacocque, pp. 232-233).

[161]We do not think that "the prince of the covenant" (v. 27) refers to the same prince as in Dan. 9:25, i.e., the Messiah and by implication, the people of God (W.H. Shea, *Selected Studies*, p. 47) or the Jerusalem High Priest (Hartman and Di Lella, p. 295). It seems to us that this interpretation does not fit the context of our verse. Several observations would rather support the idea that the prince of the covenant and the entity described in vv. 21 and 23-24 belong to the same category:

1. the parallelism found in vv. 20-22 (cf. M. Delcor, p. 233) suggests that the "be destroyed" (v. 22) should be related to the one who "shall arise in his place" in a parallel way as in v. 20.

v. 20	there shall arise in his place . . . glory (*heḏer*) of the kingdom . . . shall be destroyed (*šbr*)
v. 21	there shall arise in his place . . . honor (*hôd*) of the kingdom (v. 21) . . . shall be destroyed (*šbr*) (v. 22)

Likewise, the one "who shall come peaceably and seize the kingdom by intrigue" (v. 21) is of the same vein as the one who "shall act deceitfully" (v. 23) and "enter peaceably" (v. 24). Again the common wording suggests the same connection.

2. The association of this king with the verb "to come" (*ba'*) in vv. 11 and 24 indicates that this king belongs to the category of the *Nāgîḏ* of 9:26, the violent usurper who is also associated with the same verb "to come" rather than the *nāgîḏ* of 9:25, the Messiah (see Doukhan, "The Seventy Weeks" p. 13, n. 5 and 16).

3. The idea of covenant (*berîṯ*) which is here referred to (the last word of v. 22) should be understood in connection to

"the league" (*ḥiṯḥaberûṯ*) which is mentioned immediately afterwards (the first word of v. 23). The close association of these synonymous words suggests that the covenant and the league refer to the same thing (see Delcor, p. 235), implying therefore, that the Prince of the Covenant and of the league are related. Whenever ch. 11 refers to the covenant with a religious connotation, the latter covenant is specifically and systematically qualified as the "holy covenant" (vv. 28, 30). The other kind of covenant is simply referred to as "covenant" (vv. 22, 32, where covenant refers to the wicked, literally meaning "The wicked of the covenant;" even if in the latter verse the "holy covenant" is meant, the word "holy" has not been used, perhaps in order to avoid its inappropriate association with the word "wicked"). The expression "prince of the covenant" may well refer to a simple "confederate prince" just as in Gen. 14:13 (see Delcor, p. 235), in this instance the king of the North. Along these lines, we should then understand the "force of a flood" as a reference to his own forces (cf. 15, 31; cf. v. 26), which are devastated and broken as is the Prince of the covenant himself. Then the next verse makes sense. The king is said to come up and then he becomes strong implying the preceding stage.

[162]The expression "glory of the kingdom" is understood by most interpreters as referring to Palestine (see Lacocque, p. 225; Porteous, p. 165; Wood, p. 293). The parallelism between this expression and "the honor of the kingdom" does not necessarily exclude this interpretation (Delcor, p. 233). The two expressions come generally in pairs (Ps. 21:6; 96:6; 104:1; 111:3; Job 40:10; 1 Ch. 16:27); see esp. Ps. 145:5 where the two expressions are used together to refer to the kingdom of God (cf. v. 11).

[163]Lacocque, p. 233.

[164]Ford, p. 276; cf. Hartman and DiLella, p. 304.

[165]Cf. Hartman and DiLella, p. 304; cf. note 173.

[166]Cf. Is. 11:14 where the same order of the three countries appears within the same context of eschatology and of geographical movement.

[167]Cf. Hartman and DiLella's translation "not even the land of Egypt will escape," p. 260.

[168]The word "countries" of v. 42 points to the "countries" of v. 41 and may well, therefore, refer to the same geography, implying that Edom, Moab, and Ammon, which belong to the first "countries" also belong to the second one.

[169]M. Delcor, p. 224.

[170]Cf. Ps. 2:6, cf. M. Delcor, p. 249.

[171]See Doukhan, "The Seventy Weeks," p. 13, n. 8; cf. Hartman and DiLella, p. 305.

[172]The eschatological dimension of Daniel 11 has also been perceived by the sect of Qumran. 1 QM 1.4-7 is indeed a midrash on our text; see A. Dupont-Sommer, *The Essene Writings from Qumran*, 1973, p. 170, note 1.

[173]The North-South reference as pointing to the two extremities of the world may also convey universality, implying the totality of the world; cf. Gen. 28:14; Ps. 89:12; cf. Lacocque, p. 159. It is interesting in this connection to notice that Artaxerxes has been remembered in national Egyptian texts as "King of the South and North," implying the idea that he was the King of the totality of the world (Robert William Rogers, *A History of Ancient Persia*, 1929, p. 176).

[174]See Delcor, p. 251.

[175]See Is. 44:27, 28; cf. Jer. 50:38; cf. Herodotus I, 190, 191.

[176]The thesis "Mountain of Megiddo" which is the most defended interpretation (see e.g. Prigent, p. 249), stumbles on some difficulties, especially on the fact that there is no such mountain. The only place which would fit this name is a plain (cf. Zech. 12:11). Ch. Brutsch, who has adopted this thesis, recognizes its weakness (*Clartés sur l'Apocalypse,* 1966, p. 270. Cf. G. Schrenk, *Die Weissagung über Israel im Neuen Testament: Die Apocalypse Johannes,* n.d., p. 47). Cf. W. H. Shea, "The Location and Significance of Armageddon in Rev. 16:6," *AUSS* 18 (1980):157-162. The interpretation which reads in the word Armageddon the Greek transcription of the Hebrew *Har Mogued* (the mount of the gathering) has some supporters; cf. F. Hommell, *Neue Kirchliche Zeitschrift* 1 (1890):407ff.; Ch. C. Torrey, "Armageddon," *The Harvard Theological Review* 31 (1938):238ff. For Rissi, who sees in Revelation 16 a "proven dependence on Is. 14:13," this is up to now the most satisfactory explanation (*Was ist und was geschehen soll danach,* 1965, p. 88).

[177]See A. Robinson, "Zion and Saphon in Psalm XLVII, 3," *VT* 24 (1974):121.

[178]Jon D. Levenson, *Sinai and Zion: An Entry into the Jewish Bible,* 1985, p. 124.

[179]The connection between Dan. 11 and Rev. 16 has escaped the advocators of the Megiddo interpretation. The OT setting from which Rev. 16 would have been drawn is not the incidental episode of Elijah's sacrifice (1 Kgs. 18; see W. H. Shea, "The Location and Significance of Armageddon in Rev. 16:6," *AUSS* 18 [1980]:157-162) but the vision of Dan. 11, which also happens to deal with the same spiritual, cosmic and final conflict (see note 133).

[180]The genitive used here may well be a genitive of reference. In that case we should read "The battle with reference to the great Day of God;" cf. Heb. 3:12. See H. E. Dana and J. R. Mantey, *A Manual Grammar of the Greek New Testament,* 1955, p. 78.

[181]L. Koehler, *Old Testament Theology,* 1967, p. 88.

[182]In 2 Chron. 36, see especially v. 21, which speaks of the fulfillment of the word of God by reference to the Sabbatical year.

[183]The author of the Gospel of Matthew may well have thought of the same principle, as he started with the genealogy of Jesus, as the Old Testament does with the genealogy of Gen. 1. See G. von Rad, *Genesis*, 1961, p. 65; Doukhan, *The Genesis Creation Story*, pp. 167ff.

[184]Cf. Ps. 146-150; Ex. 15; Dan. 9; etc., where the conclusion points to the introduction; cf. especially Meir Weiss' observation on the biblical structure, pp. 271-297.

[185]Cf. Cl. Westermann, *Beginning and End in the Bible*, 1972, pp. 1, 29. Cf. also his statement, p. 37, "The central message of salvation through Jesus Christ is part of the larger context of God's word to the world. . . . Consequently, the message of salvation . . . should be only when it is accompanied by God's message concerning everything, concerning the beginning and the end."

[186]A. Neher, *The Prophetic Existence*, 1969, p. 12.

[187]*L'Epître aux Hébreux*, 1952, p. 369.

[188]See A. Vanhoye, *La Structure littéraire de L'Epître aux Hébreux*, 1963; cf. John Bligh, *Chiastic Analysis of the Epistle to the Hebrews*, 1966.

[189]Darwinism, Marxism, Spiritualism, Positivism, all these movements which started in the middle of the 19th century espoused the theories of evolution and of progress to the ideal City. The "Industrial Revolution," of what has been called "the hungry Forties," not only explains the social and political movements which took place all over Europe but it also inspired this strong emphasis on human progress (see James Laver, *Manners and Morals in the Age of Optimism 1848-1914*, 1966, p. 13; cf. George Rude, *Debate on Europe*, 1972, p. 51ff.).

[190]From a philosophical and political point of view this "urge toward unity" has been especially brandished by Hegel's idealism and in a slightly different way by Marx (see George L. Mosse, *The Culture of Western Europe: The Nineteenth and Twentieth Centuries*, 1961, pp. 142-143). Interestingly enough the same concern for unity appears in religious circles especially under the spread of foreign missions. The earliest ecumenical organized movements belong to that period (see Ch. S. McFarland, *Christian Unity in the Making*, 1948, pp. 18-19; Cf. A. T. DeGroot, *Church Unity: An Annotated Outline of the Growth of the Ecumenical Movement*, 1969, p. 3).

[191]Statistical studies have revealed that the middle of the 19th century has been characterized as being the climax of the movement of hope and waiting in religious history. See H. Desroches, *The Sociology of Hope*, 1979. Cf. J. Bach McMaster, *A History of the People of the United States*, vol. 7, New York, 1910.

[192]Ex. 15:11; Dt. 33:29; Is. 36:20; Mic. 7:17-18; Ps. 35:10; Ps. 89:9-10; Ps. 113:5-7; Job 36:22; Is. 44:7.

[193]A. Lacocque, p. 154; for the discussion on this matter see A. J. Ferch, *The Apocalyptic "Son of Man" in Daniel 7*, 1979, p. 8; for other arguments see Gerhard Hasel, "The Identity of 'the Saints of the Most High' in Daniel 7," *Biblica* 56 (1975):175-185.

[194]Gesenius, Kautzsch, Cowley, eds. *Hebrew Grammar*, 106.C.

[195]This is the third beatitude of the book of Revelation, which contains 7; note that all of them are related to the waiting (cf. 1:3; 14:13; 16:15; 19:9; 20:6; 22:7, 14).

[196]To walk naked is a technical term which means to be judged; see H. Preisker, *Theologisches Wörterbuch zum Neuen Testament*, III, 1950, p. 755. Cf. Rev. 3:18 where the same language is used, suggesting that the addressee is the same as in Rev. 16:15, namely the people of the end.

[197]Cf. T. B. Bottomore, *Elites and Society*, 1964, pp. 1-17.

[198]See Helen Flandes Dunbar, *Mind and Body: Psychosomatic Medicine*, 1955.

[199]On the influence of ethical behavior and mental balance, see especially H. Baruk, *Patients Are People Like Us*, 1978, pp. 215ff.

[200]The emphasis is on "He." The personal pronoun comes in the beginning of the sentence and is accented with the disjunctive *legarmeh*.

[201]This ritual is generally associated with mourning and death. See Lacocque, p. 182. *Taan* 16a; E. Feldman, *Biblical and Post-biblical Defilement and Mourning: Law as Theology*, 1977, pp. 71ff.

[202]G. Hasel, "Resurrection in the Theology of Old Testament Apocalyptic," *ZAW* 92 (1980):267-284.

CHRONOLOGY IN THE VISIONS OF THE END

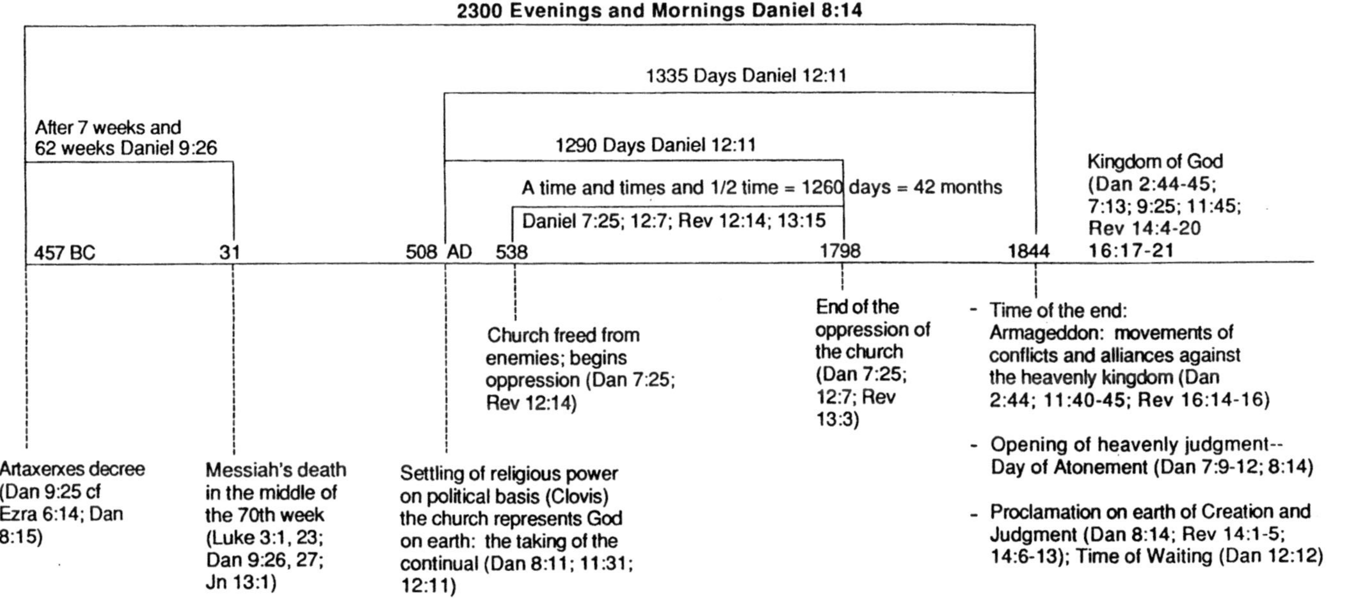

PARALLELS IN THE VISIONS OF THE END

Daniel 2: The Statue	Daniel 7: Four Beasts	Daniel 8: Two Animals	Daniel 11	Revelation 13-14	Revelation 16
vv 32a, 37, 38 Head of Gold: Babylon (603-539 BC)	v 4 Lion: Babylon			(beast evoking the beasts of Dan 7) hence the kingdoms they represent; 13:2, mouth of a lion: Babylon	
vv 32b, 39a chest and arms of silver: Medes and Persians (539-331 BC)	v 5 bear: Medes and Persians	vv 3-4 ram: Medes and Persians	v 2 Persians	13:2 feet of a bear: Medes and Persians	
vv 32c, 39b belly and thighs of bronze: Greece (331-146 BC)	v 6 leopard with 4 heads and 4 wings Greece (4 heads: division 4 kingdoms)	vv 5-8 goat: Greece (4 horns: division into 4 kingdoms)	vv 3, 4a Greece (division in 4 kingdoms)	13:2 like a leopard: Greece	
vv 3a, 40 legs of iron: Rome (146 BC-4th century AD) v 33b feet of iron and clay 3 steps v 41 1) division of the Roman Empire	vv 7, 8 cf v 19, 23 dreadful beast: Rome v 7b; cf v 24 10 horns: division of the Roman Empire	v 9a from the one of the 4 directions: Rome implied (including the period of divisions)	v 4b kingdom given to others besides these: Rome implied (including the period of divisions)	13:1 beast with 10 horns: Rome (including the period of division)	

PARALLELS IN THE VISIONS OF THE END (Continued)

v 42 2) religious power (clay) mixing with political power (iron)	v 8; cf 20b-22, 24b, 25 little horn: religious power of persecution and usurpation with regards to the law	vv 9b-13, 23-25a little horn: religious power of persecution and usurpation with regards to the law and the sanctuary	vv 5-39 war between the King of the North and the King of the South: struggles between political power and religious power, the latter being characterized as persecutor and usurper with regard to the law and the sanctuary	13:4-18 religious power of persecution and of usurpation with regard to the law and the sanctuary	
v 43 3) time of the end: tentatives of alliances in the perspective of the heavenly kingdom	vv 9-12; cf v26 judgment in heaven	v 25b time of the end: Day of Atonement in heaven	vv 40-45a time of the end: last battles alliance North and South against the heavenly kingdom	14:14-20 time of the end: a two-sided vision heavenly judgment (1-5) earthly proclamation of Creation and Judgment (point at the Day of Atonement 6-13)	v 12-16 time of the end 6th bowl: last conflict and alliance of all the powers against the coming of the heavenly kingdom (Armageddon)
vv 44-45 stone "cut out without hand": Kingdom of God	vv 13, 14 cf v 27 the Son of Man with the clouds: Kingdom of God	v 25b broken "without hands" Kingdom of God	v 45b come to his end "without help" Kingdom of God	14:14-20 the son of Man with the clouds: Kingdom of God	vv17-21 7th bowl: the coming of God

BIBLIOGRAPHY

Albright, W. F. *From the Stone Age to Christianity*. Baltimore, 1957.

Alonso Schökel, L., M. I. Gonzalez, and J. Mateos. *Daniel*. Madrid, 1976.

____________. "Hermeneutics in the Light of Language and Literature." *CBQ* 25 (1963): 378-381.

Alter, R. "A Literary Approach to the Bible." *Commentary* 60:6 (1975): 70-77.

Andersen, F. I. *The Sentence in Biblical Hebrew.* The Hague and Paris, 1974.

Archer, G. L. "The Aramaic of the 'Genesis Apocryphon' compared with the Aramaic of Daniel." In *New Perspectives on the Old Testament,* pp. 160-169. Waco, Tex., 1970.

______________. *Introduction: A Survey of Old Testament Introduction.* Chicago, 1985.

Asimov, Isaac. *The Near East: Ten Thousand Years of History.* Boston, 1968.

Avishur, Y. *Semikhuyot Hanirdafim Bameliza Hamiqrait.* Jerusalem, 1977.

Baldwin, Joyce. *Daniel: An Introduction and Commentary.* Downers Grove, Ill., 1978.

Baly, D. *God and History in the Old Testament.* New York, 1976.

Banik, H. *Patients are People Like Us.* New York, 1978.

Barr, J. "Reading the Bible as Literature." *BJRL* 56 (1973): 10-33.

Baumgartner, W. "Das Aramäische im Buche Daniel." *ZAW* 45 (1927): 81-133.

______________. *Das Buch Daniel.* Giessen, 1926.

______________. "Ein Vierteljahrhundert Danielforschung." *TRu* 11(1939): 59-83, 125-144, 201-228.

Behrmann, G. *Das Buch Daniel.* HKAT 3/3,2. Göttingen, 1894.

Bentzen, A. *Daniel.* 2nd ed. HAT 1/19. Tübingen, 1952.

Bevan, A. A. *A Short Commentary on the Book of Daniel.* Cambridge, 1892.

Bickerman, Elias. *Four Strange Books of the Bible: Jonah, Daniel, Koheleth, Esther.* New York, 1967.

Blank, S. *Prophetic Thought.* Cincinnati, Ohio, 1977.

Bligh, John. *Chiastic Analysis of the Epistle to the Hebrews.* Ovon, England, 1966.

Bloch, A. P. *The Biblical and Historical Background of Jewish Customs and Ceremonies.* New York, 1980.

Boman, T. *Hebrew Thought Compared with Greek.* London, 1960.

Bottomore, T. B. *Elites and Society.* New York, 1964.

Boutflower, C. *In and Around the Book of Daniel.* Grand Rapids, Mich., 1964.

Bowman, R. A. "The North Country." *IDB* (1962): 560.

Braude, W. G., tr. *The Midrash on Psalms.* Vol. 1. Yale Judaica Series 13. Yale, 1959.

Bright, J. *A History of Israel.* Philadelphia, 1981.

Brongers, H. A. "Die Zehnzahl in der Bibel und ihrer Umwelt." In *Studia Biblica et Semitica: Festschrift Th. C. Vriezen,* pp. 20-45. Wageningen, 1966.

Brown, F., S. R. Driver, and C. A. Briggs. *A Hebrew and English Lexicon of the Old Testament.* Oxford, 1907.

Brown, R. E. *The Book of Daniel*. New York, 1962.

_____________. "The Pre-Christian Semitic Concept of Mystery." *CBQ* 20 (1958): 417-443.

Bruce, F. F. "The Book of Daniel and the Qumran Community." In *Neotestamentica et Semitica: Studies in Honour of Matthew Black*, pp. 221-235. Edinburgh, 1969.

Brutsch, Ch. *Clartés sur l'Apocalypse*. Geneva, 1966.

Caquot, A. "Sur les quatre bêtes de *Daniel* VII." *Sem* 5 (1955): 5-13.

_____________. "Les quatre bêtes et le 'Fils d'homme' (Daniel 7)." *Sem* 17 (1968): 37-71.

Casey, M. "The Corporate Interpretation of 'One Like a Son of Man' (Dan. VII 13) at the Time of Jesus." *NovT* 18 (1976): 167-180.

_____________. "Porphyry and the Origin of the Book of Daniel." *JTS* 27 (1976): 15-33.

Ceresko, R. "The Chiastic Word Pattern in Hebrew." *CBQ* (1976): 303-311.

Charles, R. H. *Eschatology: The Doctrine of a Future Life in Israel, Judaism and Christianity*. Introduction by G.W. Buchanan. New York, 1963.

Childs, B. S. *Biblical Theology in Crisis*. Philadelphia, 1970.

_____________. *Introduction to the Old Testament as Scripture*. Philadelphia, 1979.

Church, W. F. *The Influence of the Enlightenment on the French Revolution*. Lexington, Mass., 1974.

Clifford, Richard J. *The Cosmic Mountain, in Canaan and the Old Testament.* Cambridge, Mass., 1972.

____________. "History and Myth in Daniel 10-12." *BASOR* 220 (1975): 23-26.

Coggins, R. J. · *The First and Second Book of Chronicles.* New York, 1976.

Cole, R. A. *Exodus.* London, 1973.

Collins, J. J. "Apocalyptic Eschatology as the Transcendence of Death." *CBQ* 36 (1974): 21-43.

____________. "The Son of Man and the Saints of the Most High in the Book of Daniel." *JBL* 93 (1974): 50-66.

____________. "The Symbolism of Transcendence in Jewish Apocalyptic." *BR* 19 (1974): 5-22.

Congar, Y. *L'Eglise de St. Augustin à l'époque moderne.* Paris, 1976.

Coppens, J. "La mention d'un Fils de l'homme angélique en Ap.14:14." In *L'Apocalypse johannique et l'Apocalyptique dans le Nouveau Testament*, p. 229. Ed. J. Lambrecht. Louvain, 1980.

____________. "Le Fils d'homme danièlique et les relectures de Dan. vii, 13, dans les apocryphes et les écrits du Nouveau Testament." *ETL* 37 (1961): 5-51.

Cullman, O. *Christ and Time.* Philadelphia, 1962.

____________. *The Christology of the New Testament.* Philadelphia, 1959.

Dahood, M. *Psalms.* AB. New York, 1966.

Dana, H. E., and J. R. Montey, *A Manual Grammar of the Greek New Testament.* Toronto, 1955.

DeGroot, A. T. *Church Unity: An Annotated Outline of the Growth of the Ecumenical Movement.* Fort Worth, Tex., 1969.

Delcor, M. *Le Livre de Daniel.* Paris, 1971.

_____________. "Les sources du chapitre VII de Daniel." *VT* 18 (1968): 290-312.

Desroche, H. *The Sociology of Hope.* Boston, 1979.

DiLella, A. A. "The Problem of Retribution in the Wisdom Literature." In *Rediscovery of Scripture: Biblical Theology Today,* pp. 109-127. Burlington, Wis., 1967.

Doukhan, Jacques B. "Anthroponymie biblique et prophétie." Master's thesis, University of Strasbourg, 1971.

_____________. *Aux portes de l'Espérance.* Dammarie-les-Lys, France, 1983.

_____________. *Drinking at the Sources.* Mountain View, Calif., 1981.

_____________. *The Genesis Creation Story: Its Literary Structure.* Berrien Springs, Mich., 1978.

_____________. "The Seventy Weeks of Daniel 9: An Exegetical Study." *AUSS* 17 (1979): 1-21.

Driver, G. R. "The Aramaic of the Book of Daniel." *JBL* 45 (1926): 110-119.

Driver, S. R. *The Book of Daniel.* Cambridge, England, 1922.

Dunbar, Helen Handes. *Mind and Body: Psychosomatic Medicine.* New York, 1955.

Dupont-Sommer, A. *The Essene Writings from Qumran.* Gloucester, Mass., 1973.

Entsiklopedia Miqraith. Vol. 3. Jerusalem, 1965.

Feldman, E. *Biblical and Post-Biblical Defilement and Mourning: Law as Theology.* New York, 1977.

Ferch, A. J. *'Son of Man' in Daniel 7.* Berrien Springs, Mich., 1979.

Feuillet, A. "Le fils de l'homme de Daniel et la tradition biblique." *RB* 60 (1953): 170-202, 321-346.

Flusser, D. "The Four Empires in the Fourth Sibyl and in the Book of Daniel." *Israel Oriental Studies* 2 (1972): 148-175.

Fohrer, Georg. *Hebrew and Aramaic Dictionary of the Old Testament.* London, 1973.

Ford, Desmond. *Daniel.* Nashville, Tenn., 1978.

Froom, L. E. *The Prophetic Faith of Our Fathers.* Washington, D.C., 1950.

Frost, S. B. *Old Testament Apocalyptic: Its Origins and Growth.* London, 1952.

Gage, W. A. *The Gospel of Genesis.* Winona Lake, Ind., 1984.

Ganzfried S. *Code of Jewish Law.* New York, 1963.

Gesenius, F., E. Kautzsch, and A. E. Cowley. *Hebrew Grammar.* Oxford, 1910.

Gilbert, M. "La prière de Daniel: Dn 9, 4-19." *RTL* 3 (1972): 284-310.

Ginsberg, H. L. "The Composition of the Book of Daniel." *VT* 4 (1954): 246-275.

_____________. *Studies in Daniel.* New York, 1948.

Ginsburg, C. D. *Introduction to the Massoretico-Critical Edition of the Hebrew Bible.* London, 1897.

Ginzberg, L. "Daniel." In *The Jewish Encyclopedia,* 4:426-428. Ed. I. Singer. New York, 1903.

Goldwurm, Hersh. *Daniel: A New Translation with a Commentary Anthologized from Talmudic, Midrashic and Rabbinic Sources.* New York, 1979.

Goudoever, Van J. *Fêtes et calendriers bibliques.* Paris, 1967.

Grelot, P. "Soixante-dix semaines d'années." *Bib* 50 (1969): 169-186.

Griffin, William. *Endtime: The Doomsday Catalog.* New York, 1979.

Gruenthaner, M. J. "The Four Empires of Daniel." *CBQ* 8 (1946): 72-82, 201-212.

Hals, R. M. *Grace and Faith in the Old Testament.* Minneapolis, Minn., 1980.

Hammer, R. *The Book of Daniel.* The Cambridge Bible Commentary, NEB. New York: Cambridge University Press, 1976.

Hardy, F. N. *An Historical Perspective in Daniel II.* Berrien Springs, Mich., 1983.

Hartill, J. E. *Biblical Hermeneutics.* Grand Rapids, Mich., 1960.

Hartman, L. F. "The Great Tree and Nabuchodonosor's Madness." In *The Bible in Current Catholic Thought,* pp. 75-82. New York, 1962.

Hartman, L. F., and A. DiLella. *The Book of Daniel.* AB. Garden City, N.Y., 1978.

Hartom, E. S. *Daniel.* Tel Aviv, 1973.

Hasel, Gerhard. "The Identity of 'the Saints of the Most High' in Daniel 7." *Biblica* 56 (1975): 175-185.

______________. "Problem of the Center in the Old Testament Debate." *ZAW* 86 (1976): 65-82.

______________. "Is the Aramaic of Daniel Early or Late?" *Ministry* (Jan. 1980), pp. 12-13.

______________. "Resurrection in the Theology of Old Testament Apocalyptic." *ZAW* 92 (1980): 267-284.

______________. "The 'Little Horn,' the Saints, and the Sanctuary in Daniel 8." In *The Sanctuary and the Atonement*, pp. 177-227. Washington, D.C., 1981.

______________. "Studies in Biblical Atonement II: The Day of Atonement." In *The Sanctuary and the Atonement*, pp. 115-156. Washington, D.C., 1981.

______________. *Old Testament Theology: Basic Issues in the Current Debate.* Grand Rapids, Mich., 1985.

Heschel, A. *The Sabbath: Its Meaning for Modern Man.* New York, 1976.

Hitti, Philip. *The Near East in History: A 5000 Year Story.* Princeton, N.J., 1961.

Horn, S. H., and L. S. Wood. *The Chronology of Ezra 7.* Washington, D.C., 1953.

Hrubi, K. "Le Yom ha-kippurim ou Jour de l'Expiation." *Or Syr* 10 (1965): 181-192.

Humphreys, W. L. *The Motif of the Wise Courtier in the Old Testament.* New York, 1970.

Jackson, J., and M. Kessler. *Rhetorical Criticism: Essays in Honour of J. Muilenburg.* Theological Essays, Series 1. Pittsburgh, Pa., 1974.

Jastrow, M. *A Dictionary of the Targumim, the Talmud Babli and Yerushalmi, and the Midrashic Literature.* New York, 1963.

Jeffery, Arthur. *The Book of Daniel: Introduction and Exegesis.* IB6. New York, 1956.

Johnsson, W. G. "Defilement and Purgation in the Book of Hebrews." Ph.D. diss., Vanderbilt University, 1973.

Jones, B. W. "The Prayer in Daniel IX." *VT* 18 (1968): 488-493.

Josephus, F. *Jewish Antiquities*, IX-XI. Boston, 1958.

Kaufmann, Y. *The Religion of Israel, from its Beginning to the Babylonian Exile.* London, 1960.

Kearney, Peter J. "Creation and Liturgy: The P Redaction of Exodus 25-40." *ZAW* 89 (1977): 375-387.

Keil, C. F. *The Book of the Prophet Daniel.* Tr. M.G. Easton. Edinburgh, 1884.

Keil, C. F. *The Pentateuch*. II. Grand Rapids, Mich., n.d.; reprint ed. of 1875.

Kessler, M. "New Directions in Biblical Exegesis." *Scottish Journal of Theology* 24 (1971): 317-325.

King, Geoffrey R. *Daniel*. Grand Rapids, Mich., 1966.

Kitchen, K. A. *Notes on Some Problems in the Book of Daniel*. London, 1965.

Koehler, L. *Old Testament Theology*. Philadelphia, 1967.

Koehler, L., and W. Baumgartner. *Lexicon in Veteris Testamenti Libros*. Leiden, 1958.

Kuhn, K. G. "Babylon." In *Theological Dictionary of the New Testament*. Ed. Gerhard Kittel. Grand Rapids, Mich., 1964.

Kutscher, E. Y. "Aramaic." In *Current Trends in Linguistics*. Vol. 6: *Linguistics in South West Asia and North Africa*, pp. 347-412. The Hague, 1970.

____________ "Ha Aramit ha Miqrait Aramit Mizrahit hi o Maaravit?" In *First World Congress of Jewish Studies*, vol. 1, pp. 123-127. Jerusalem, 1952.

Lacocque, A. *The Book of Daniel*. Atlanta, 1979.

Ladd, G. E. *Crucial Questions About the Kingdom of God*. Grand Rapids, Mich., 1952.

Lange, J. P. *The Revelation of John: A Commentary on the Holy Scriptures*. Vol. 10. New York, 1874.

LaRondelle, H. K. *The Israel of God in Prophecy*. Berrien Springs, Mich., 1983.

LaRondelle, H. K. *Perfection and Perfectionism*. Berrien Springs, Mich., 1975.

Laver, James. *Manners and Morals in the Age of Optimism*. New York, 1966.

Lengler, A. "La Structure Littéraire de Daniel 2-7." *Bib* 53 (1972): 169-190.

Leupold, Herbert C. *Exposition of Daniel*. Grand Rapids, Mich., 1969.

Levenson, Jon D. *Sinai and Zion: An Entry into the Jewish Bible*. Minneapolis, Minn., 1985.

Lohmeyer, E. *Die Offenbarung des Johannes*. Handbuch zum Neuen Testament 16. 2nd ed. Tübingen, 1953.

Marco, A. de. "Der Chiasmus in der Bibel: Ein Beitrag zur strukturellen Stilistik." *Linguistica Biblica* 36 (1975): 21-97; 37 (1976): 31-68.

Martin-Archard, Robert. *Essai biblique sur les fêtes d'Israël*. Geneva, 1979.

McCullough, W. S. "Israel's Eschatology from Amos to Daniel." In *Studies in the Ancient Palestinian World*, pp. 86-100. Eds. J. W. Wevers and D. B. Redford. Toronto, 1972.

McFarland, Ch. S. *Christian Unity in the Making*. New York, 1948.

McMaster, J. Bach. *A History of the People of the United States from the Revolution to the Civil War*. Vol. 7. New York, 1910.

Melamed, E. Z. *Mefarshe Hamiqra*. Vol. 2. Jerusalem, 1973.

Melugin, R. F. "Muilenburg, Form Criticism, and Theological Exegesis." In *Encounter with the Text*, pp. 91-102. Ed. M. Buss. Semeia Supplements 8. Philadelphia, 1979.

Mickelsen, A. Berkeley. *Interpreting the Bible*. Grand Rapids, Mich., 1963.

Miqraoth Gdoloth. Tel Aviv, 1959.

Mitchell, T.C., and R. Joice. "The Musical Instruments in Nebuchadnezzar's Orchestra." In *Notes on Some Problems in the Book of Daniel*, pp. 19-27. London, 1965.

Montgomery, J. A. *The Book of Daniel*. ICC. New York, 1927.

____________. *A Critical and Exegetical Commentary on the Book of Daniel*. Edinburgh, 1950.

Mosse, George L. *The Culture of Western Europe: The Nineteenth and Twentieth Centuries*. Chicago, 1961.

Mowinckel, S. *He That Cometh*. Tr. G. W. Anderson. Nashville, Tenn., 1956.

Müller, U. B. *Messias und Menschensohn in Jüdischen Apokalypsen und in der Offenbarung des Johannes*. Gütersloh, 1972.

Muraoka, T. "Notes on the Syntax of Biblical Aramaic." *JSS* 11 (1966): 151-167.

Murska, T. "The Aramaic of the Old Targum of Job from Qumran Cave XI." *Journal of Jewish Studies* 25 (1974): 424-443.

Neher, André. *The Prophetic Existence*. South Brunswick, N.J., 1969.

Nickelsburg, G. W. E. *Resurrection, Immortality, and Eternal Life in Intertestamental Judaism.* HTS 26. Cambridge, Mass., 1972.

Noth, M. *The Laws in the Pentateuch and Other Essays.* Philadelphia, 1967.

Pedersen, J. *Israel, Its Life and Culture.* 2 vols. London, 1959.

Pinches, Theophilus G. *An Outline of Assyrian Grammar.* London, 1910.

Plöger, Otto. *Das Buch Daniel.* Gütersloh, 1965.

Pope, M. H. *'El' in the Ugaritic Texts.* Leiden, 1955.

____________. *Job.* Garden City, N.Y., 1972.

____________. "Number, Numbering, Numbers." *IDB* (1962): 561-567.

Porteous, N.W. *Daniel.* Philadelphia, 1965.

Preisker, H. *Theologisches Wörterbuch zum Neuen Testament.* Vol. 3. Stuttgart, 1950.

Price, G. McCready. *The Time of the End.* Nashville, Tenn., 1967.

Prigent, P. *L'Apocalypse de Saint Jean.* Paris, 1981.

Pritchard, James B., ed. *Ancient Near Eastern Texts Relating to the Old Testament.* Princeton, 1950.

Rad, G. von. *Old Testament Theology.* New York, 1965.

____________. *The Problem of the Hexateuch and Other Essays.* New York, 1966.

Rahlfs, A., ed. *Septuaginta.* Vol. 2. Stuttgart, 1935.

Rawlinson, George. *The Five Great Monarchies of the Ancient World.* New York, 1887.

Redford, D. B. *A Study of the Biblical Story of Joseph (Genesis 37-50).* VTSup. 20. Leiden, 1970.

Rissi, M. *Was ist und was geschehen soll danach.* Zurich, 1965.

Robinson, A. "Zion and Saphon in Psalm XLVII, 3." *VT* 24 (1974):118-127.

Rogers, Robert William. *A History of Ancient Persia, from the Earliest Beginnings to the Death of Alexander the Great.* New York, 1929.

Rosen, H. B. "On the Use of the Tenses in the Aramaic of Daniel." *JSS* 6 (1961): 183-203.

Rosenthal, F. *A Grammar of Biblical Aramaic.* Wiesbaden, 1983.

Rowley, H. H. "The Meaning of Daniel for Today: A Study of Leading Themes." *Int* 15 (1961): 387-430.

____________. "The Unity of the Book of Daniel." In *The Servant of the Lord and Other Essays on the Old Testament,* pp. 249-280. 2nd ed. Oxford, 1965.

Rude, George. *Debate on Europe.* New York, 1972.

Russel, D. S. *The Method and Message of Jewish Apocalyptic 200 B.C. - A.D. 100.* London, 1964.

Sanders, J. A. *Torah and Canon.* Philadelphia, 1979.

Sandmel, Samuel. "Parallelomania." *JBL* 81 (1962): 1-13.

Schedl, C. "Mystische Arithmetik oder geschichtliche Zahlen (Dan. 8:14; 12:11-13)." *BZ* 8 (1964): 101-105.

Scherman, N., and M. Zlotowitz. *Daniel.* New York, 1979.

Schrenk, G. *Die Weissagung über Israel im Neuen Testament: Die Apocalypse Johannes.* Zurich, n.d.

Seebass, H. "Acharith." In *Theological Dictionary of the Old Testament,* 1:207-212. Ed. G. Johannes Botterweck and H. Ringgren. Grand Rapids, Mich., 1986.

Sellin, E. *Theologie des Alten Testaments.* Leipzig, 1936.

Shea, W. H. *Selected Studies on Prophetic Interpretation.* Washington, D.C., 1982.

____________. "Unity of Daniel." In *Symposium on Daniel,* pp. 165-255. Washington, D.C., 1986.

Sherman, N., and M. Zlotowitz. *Daniel.* New York, 1979.

Siegman, E. F. "The Stone Hewn from the Mountain (Daniel 2)." *CBQ* 18 (1956): 364-379.

Silberman, L. H. "The Human Deed in a Time of Despair: The Ethics of Apocalyptic." In *Essays in Old Testament Ethics (J. Philip Hyatt: In Memorandiam),* pp. 191-202. Eds. J. L. Crenshaw and J. T. Willis. New York, 1974.

Soden, W. von. *Akkadisches Handwörterbuch.* Wiesbaden, 1965.

Spiegel, S. "Noah, Daniel, and Job." In *Louis Ginzberg Jubilee Volume,* pp. 305-355. New York, 1945.

Strand, K. O. *Interpreting the Book of Revelation.* Worthington, Ohio, 1976.

Strauss, L. *Bedarkhe Hasifrut.* Jerusalem, 1959.

Thiele, Ed. R. *A Chronology of the Hebrew Kings.* Grand Rapids, Mich., 1977.

Thucydides. *History of the Peloponnesian War.* Trans. from the Greek by William Smith. New York, 1961.

Torrance, F. *Royal Priesthood.* Edinburgh, 1955.

Torrey, C. C. "Notes on the Aramaic Part of Daniel." *Connecticut Academy of Arts and Sciences Transactions* 15 (1909): 241-282.

Towner, W. S. "The Poetic Passages of Daniel 1-6." *CBQ* 31 (1969): 317-326.

Ullmann, W. *Principles of Government and Politics in the Middle Ages.* New York, 1961.

Ulmer, F. *Die semitischen Eigennamen im Alten Testament.* Leipzig, 1901.

Vanhoye, A. *La structure littéraire de l'épître aux Hébreux.* Paris, 1963.

Vaux, R. de. *Ancient Israel: Its Life and Institutions.* New York, 1961.

Vawter, B. "Apocalyptic: Its Relation to Prophecy. " *CBQ* 22 (1960): 33-46.

Vriezen, T. C. *An Outline of Old Testament Theology.* Newton, Mass., 1970.

Walzel, O. *Gehalt und Gestalt im Kunstwerk des Dichters.* Darmstadt, 1957.

Weil, E. *Choulkhâne Aroukh Abrégé.* Strasbourg, 1948.

Weiss, Meir. *Hamiqra Ki-demuto*. Jerusalem, 1962.

____________. *The Bible from Within*. Jerusalem, 1986.

Welch, A. C. *Visions of the End: A Study of Daniel and Revelation*. Boston, 1922.

____________. *The Work of the Chronicler*. London, 1939.

Wenham, G. J. *The Book of Leviticus*. Grand Rapids, Mich., 1979.

Westermann, Claus. *Beginning and End in the Bible*. Philadelphia, 1972.

____________. "Sinn und Grenze religionsgeschichtlicher Parallelen." *Theologische Literaturzeitung* 90 (1965): 490-491.

Wheelwright, P. *Metaphor and Reality*. Bloomington, Ind., 1962.

Whitcomb, J. C. *Darius the Mede: A Study in Historical Identification*. Grand Rapids, Mich., 1959.

Wilder, A. N. "The Rhetoric of Ancient and Modern Apocalyptic." *Int* 25 (1971): 436-453.

Wilson, R. D. "The Book of Daniel and the Canon." *Princeton Theological Review* 13 (1915): 352-408.

Wood, L. *A Commentary on Daniel*. Grand Rapids, Mich., 1976.

Wolf, C. U. "Daniel and the Lord's Prayer: A Synthesis of the Theology of the Book of Daniel." *Int* 15 (1961): 398-410.

Yamauchi, E. M. *Greece and Babylon*. Grand Rapids, Mich., 1967.

Yeivin, Israel. *Introduction to the Tiberian Masorah*. Missoula, Mont., 1980.

Yellin, D. *Ketavim Nivharim*. 2 vols. Jerusalem, 1939.

Zimmerli, W. *Man and His Hope in the Old Testament*. London, 1968.

_____________. "Promise and Fulfillment." In *Essays on Old Testament Hermeneutics*, pp. 89-122. Ed. by C. Westermann. Richmond, Va., 1963.

Zöckler, Otto. "The Book of the Prophet Daniel." In *A Commentary on the Holy Scriptures*. Vol. 13. Ed. John P. Lange. New York, 1915.

INDEX

A

E

F

G

H